CAROLING TO CHRISTMAS

A Christmas Devotional in Carols, Hymns & Songs

Edited by

Bradley W. Maston

and E Dane Rogers

TRUE
GRACE
BOOKS

Published by True Grace Books

Vashon, WA

D1490583

TRUE GRACE BOOKS

Caroling to Christmas: A Christmas Devotional in
    Carols, Hymns & Songs

Copyright © 2023 by True Grace Books

True Grace Books, *Vashon, WA*

Published by True Grace Books LLC

Caroling to Christmas: A Devotional in Christmas Carols
    / Edited by Bradley W. Maston and E Dane
    Rogers.

   Library of Congress Control Number: 2023920779

ISBN: 978-1-7327779-5-8

1. Christmas.   2. Devotions.   3. Hymns, carols

Cover design by E Dane Rogers
Graphics by Canva, licensed use

CAROLING to CHRISTMAS

A Christmas Devotional in
Carols, Hymns & Songs

Forward

Many people sacrificially gave their time to make this little volume possible. It has been a gift to see such amazing teachers of God's word gather around the miracle of Christ's first arrival on Earth. I am blessed to count each of them as friends, for it is a wonderful gift to be surrounded by such admirable followers of Jesus Christ.

This format is unfamiliar to most contributors. They are used to writing great treatises and preparing lengthy articles and books. That makes this devotional so precious. We get to see the warm devotional heart of those who may often appear as purely intellectual giants of the faith.

These theologians spend their lives examining Scripture. To examine the poetic lyrics is a step out of their normal comfort zone. This has lent to a fresh look into the wonder of Christmas. We are touched by the poetry and the music that informs our view of this remarkable moment in history.

Dear reader, please enjoy this humble volume. Much love and care, hours of editing, typesetting, and prayer all led to its existence. I am most humbled and thankful for the hours of effort that were given to accomplish one simple task: To help you keep your eyes on Jesus this Christmas.

Merry Christmas,
Bradley W. Maston, PhD

Preface

I am ashamed to admit that I have been a grinch. As a young man out in the workforce, making very little money, and the victim of horrible companies which would feign to give even a day off for Christmas, and that without any pay. I saw the materialism, the ugliness, and the stress of the holiday far outweighing any benefits. The words of Ebeneezer Scrooge echoed in my ears as I struggled to provide for a young family:

"Christmas a humbug, uncle!" said Scrooge's nephew. "You don't mean that, I am sure?"

"I do," said Scrooge. "Merry Christmas! What right have you to be merry? What reason have you to be merry? You're poor enough."

"Come, then," returned the nephew gaily. "What right have you to be dismal? What reason have you to be morose? You're rich enough."

Scrooge having no better answer ready on the spur of the moment, said, "Bah!" again; and followed it up with "Humbug."

"Don't be cross, uncle!" said the nephew. "What else can I be," returned the uncle, "when I live in such a world of fools as this? Merry Christmas! Out upon merry Christmas! What's Christmas time to you but a time for paying bills without money; a time for finding yourself a year older, but not an hour richer; a time for balancing your books and having every item in 'em through a round dozen of months presented dead against you? If I could work my will," said Scrooge indignantly, "every idiot who goes about with 'Merry Christmas' on his lips, should be boiled with his own pudding, and buried with a stake of holly through his heart. He should!"[1]

Not so long later I was given the great honor of being brought on as the pastor of Fort Collins Bible Church. Yet, now Christmas seemed just as much a trial. Christmas parties, events, and other such distractions breaking up my sermon series and keeping people from our regular studies and services.

This was the way of things until a kindly friend at our church explained to me, "I used to feel the same way, but then I realized that whatever Christmas means to everyone else, to me it will only be about Jesus Christ, and how much He loved us." After those words I became a repentant and reformed grinch. No longer hearing the words of Ebeneezer Scrooge I finally heard the words of his good nephew, Fred:

---

[1] Dickens, Charles. *Works of Charles Dickens (200+ Works) The Adventures of Oliver Twist, Great Expectations, A Christmas Carol, A Tale of Two Cities, Bleak House, David Copperfield & more* (mobi). Kindle Edition.

"There are many things from which I might have derived good, by which I have not profited, I dare say," returned the nephew. "Christmas among the rest. But I am sure I have always thought of Christmas time, when it has come round--apart from the veneration due to its sacred name and origin, if anything belonging to it can be apart from that--as a good time; a kind, forgiving, charitable, pleasant time; the only time I know of, in the long calendar of the year, when men and women seem by one consent to open their shut-up hearts freely, and to think of people below them as if they really were fellow-passengers to the grave, and not another race of creatures bound on other journeys. And therefore, uncle, though it has never put a scrap of gold or silver in my pocket, I believe that it has done me good, and will do me good; and I say, God bless it!"[2]

I hope that this little daily reader will do the same for you. Keeping Christ at the center of Christmas is the only way that we can truly enjoy the blessings of this season. May these words help you to think seriously upon the great hymns of Christmas and all that they teach us about the amazing love of Jesus Christ.

---

[2] Dickens, Charles. *Works of Charles Dickens*.

DECEMBER 1

Good Christian Men Rejoice

By Clay Ward

Good Christian Men Rejoice

Good Christian Men rejoice
with heart and soul and voice;
Give we heed to what we say:
News, News, Jesus Christ is born today!
Ox and ass before him bow,
and He is in the manger now
Christ is born today,
Christ is born today.

God Christian Men rejoice
with heart and soul and voice,
Now ye hear of endless bliss,
 Joy! Joy! Jesus Christ was born for this.
He hath ope'd the heavenly door,
and man is blessed ever more;
Christ was born for this!
Christ was born for this.

Good Christian Men rejoice
with heart and soul and voice,
Now ye need not fear the grave. Peace! Peace!
Jesus Christ was born to save!
Calls you one, calls you all,
to gain His everlasting hall;
Christ was born to save!
Christ was born to save!

Many Christmas hymns picture the biblical scene of angels appearing to the shepherds in the field: *Angels We have Heard on High, It Came Upon the Midnight Clear, Hark! The Herald Angels Sing, O Come All Ye Faithful*, and *Good Christian Men Rejoice* among others. How fascinating that God delivered the birth announcement of the Savior to the shepherds, a group of people looked down upon by society due to their despised job—but honored by God with this most exciting news. God selected these hardworking men to be the first witnesses of the fact Messiah had come.

Good Christian Men Rejoice, a heartening carol about the angelic visit to the shepherds, was written by Heinrich Suso, a man born to privilege in 1295 who chose to devote his life to the Lord's service as a Dominican Monk. During that time, Suso wrote *The Little Book of Truth*, a defense of making the Gospel more presentable to the masses. This bold move of going against tradition landed him on trial for heresy and eventually sent him into exile in Switzerland, a most humiliating punishment for a man of privilege.

One night while in exile, Suso had a dream where angels invited him to rejoice. This dream motivated Suso to write *Good Christian Men Rejoice*. However, he wrote it in such a way that he went against all the rules of hymn writing in the 14th century. At the time, hymns were not written in the people's common language; were based totally on Scripture; and took a solemn tone, but Suso's hymn challenges the singer to rejoice over the incredible news of the birth of the Messiah.

In the 1800s, James Mason Neale, who shared a kindred spirit with Suso for going against the norm, put Suso's joyous work to music. Neale too was exiled and faced great persecution for his concern for the spiritually lost. The zeal of both men to reach unbelievers for Christ resulted in a most beloved hymn that celebrates the coming of Christ, the Savior of mankind. Eventually, Suso, who was persecuted in life, was posthumously recognized for his contribution to the body of Christ when in 1831, nearly five hundred years after Suso's death, the Catholic Pope declared Suso a saint.

Suso's famous hymn calls for "good Christian men" to rejoice. The call seemingly comes from the angelic host and reflects the events of Luke 2 where the shepherds are exhorted by the angels to seek Jesus, born and lying in a manger. Likely watching the sheep used in the Temple sacrifices, these shepherds saw the glory of the Lord appear to them, an awesome reason for rejoicing!

The understanding that all creation worships the One born and lying in the manger is emphasized in the second verse of Suso's hymn. That One, born in Bethlehem so long ago, is the very Creator who entered the fallen world for the purpose of redeeming it from sin. With the birth of the Savior, the Prince of peace, the One who makes the peaceful relationship with God, comes the opportunity for "endless bliss" to all who choose to believe in Him for the forgiveness of sin. Such information is News indeed!

Luke records that the shepherds responded with faith and quickly went to see the child in the manger. Upon their return to the fields, they were the first evangelists with a focused message on the Savior of mankind and the access to Heaven that He makes possible. Suso encourages rejoicing with the shepherds in the reality that the opening of the "heavenly door" is only through Jesus Christ, the One "born for this."

The third verse highlights the removal of the fear of death upon faith acceptance of Christ's peace. The call for salvation goes out to all, but sadly not all will respond, choosing instead to remain in their state of hostility to God rather than accepting the peace that Jesus brings. You do not have to fear death or be at enmity with God; you can be saved by believing in Jesus Christ who was born to die for your sins.

Like the shepherds long ago, we still have the same Good News to sing about with great joy. Jesus is no longer in the manger but has died on the cross for our sins and resurrected from the dead by the power of God. "Good Christian men" awaiting Jesus' return possess the foundation for joy having peace with God through Jesus Christ. So, in the words of Suso, "Good Christian men, rejoice!"

Luke 2:8-21

In the same region there were some shepherds staying out in the fields and keeping watch over their flock by night. And an angel of the Lord suddenly stood before them, and the glory of the Lord shone around them; and they were terribly frightened. But the angel said to them, "Do not be afraid; for behold, I bring you good news of great joy which will be for all the people; for today in the city of David there has been born for you a Savior, who is Christ the Lord. "This will be a sign for you: you will find a baby wrapped in cloths and lying in a manger." And suddenly there appeared with the angel a multitude of the heavenly host praising God and saying, "Glory to God in the highest, And on earth peace among men with whom He is pleased."

When the angels had gone away from them into heaven, the shepherds began saying to one another, "Let us go straight to Bethlehem then, and see this thing that has happened which the Lord has made known to us." So they came in a hurry and found their way to Mary and Joseph, and the baby as He lay in the manger. When they had seen this, they made known the statement which had been told them about this Child. And all who heard it wondered at the things which were told them by the shepherds. But Mary treasured all these things, pondering them in her heart. The shepherds went back, glorifying and praising God for all that they had heard and seen, just as had been told them.

DECEMBER 2

Angels We Have Heard on High

By Dr. Bradley W. Maston

Angels We Have Heard on High

Angels we have heard on high,
sweetly singing o'er the plains,
and the mountains in reply
echoing their joyous strains:

Gloria, in excelsis Deo!
Gloria, in excelsis Deo!

Shepherds, why this jubilee?
Why your joyous strains prolong?
What the gladsome tidings be
which inspire your heav'nly song?

Come to Bethlehem and see
Him whose birth the angels sing;
come, adore on bended knee
Christ the Lord, the new-born King.

See within a manger laid
Jesus, Lord of heav'n and earth!
Mary, Joseph, lend your aid,
sing with us our Savior's birth.

T his great song always reminds me of Linus Van Pelt. At the climax of the Peanuts' Christmas Carol Linus gives a speech explaining what Christmas is really about:

"Sure, Charlie Brown, I can tell you what Christmas is all about," said Linus. [Linus walks to center stage.]

"Lights, please."

And there were in the same country shepherds abiding in the field, keeping watch over their flock by night. And, lo, the angel of the Lord came upon them, and the glory of the Lord shone round about them: and they were sore afraid. And the angel said unto them, Fear not: for, behold, I bring you good tidings of great joy, which shall be to all people. For unto you is born this day in the city of David a Savior, which is Christ the Lord. And this shall be a sign unto you; Ye shall find the babe wrapped in swaddling clothes, lying in a manger. And suddenly there was with the angel a multitude of the heavenly host praising God, and saying, Glory to God in the highest, and on earth peace, goodwill toward men.

[Linus picks up his blanket and shuffles off-stage.]

"That's what Christmas is all about,
Charlie Brown."

This remarkable and well-loved Christmas hymn gets us all to sing in Latin each year, which is no small accomplishment. As we sing *"glo–ooo–oh–ooo–oh–ooo–oria, in excelsis Deo"* we may wonder what we are saying. The "Gloria" we can figure out is "glory". "Deo" is clearly "God". That leaves "in excelsis"— which means "in the highest". We are singing the words that the angels spoke, and it works so much better with this melody than the English translation, though I urge you to try it.

This hymn returns after each verse to remind us of this important point: That God was glorified in Christ's coming to the earth. What Philippians 2 describes so graphically as Christ humbling himself to take on human form and suffer on our behalf is here noted as bringing glory to God in the highest! In Christ's coming to earth, peace was brought to us and made available to us by receiving His free gift of forgiveness and salvation (Rom. 5:1).

This hymn draws our attention to the other actors. The angels were given the honorable mission to announce the Messiah's birth to shepherds in a field at night. The shepherds heard the message and ran to Bethlehem to behold the Christ-child. The tender mission of Mary and Joseph to provide for the Baby Jesus a humble trough for feeding animals. This beautiful song brings us to the best of the Christmas season.

We have the choice to sing the glory of God because of what Jesus Christ did for us. We have the opportunity to race to the feet of Jesus and fix our gaze upon Him (Heb. 12:1–2), as the shepherds had done. We have the opportunity to make the humble circumstances of our lives a place that, though not worthy of Him apart from His work, welcomes Jesus Christ our Savior.

1 Peter 1:12

"To them it was revealed that, not to themselves, but to us they were ministering the things which now have been reported to you through those who have preached the gospel to you by the Holy Spirit sent from heaven—things which angels desire to look into."

DECEMBER 3

Joy to the World

By Jeremy Thomas

Joy to the World

Joy to the world! the Lord is come;
Let Earth receive her King;
Let every heart prepare him room,
And heaven and nature sing,
And heaven and nature sing,
And heaven, and heaven, and nature sing.

No more let sins and sorrows grow,
Nor thorns infest the ground;
He comes to make His blessings flow
Far as the curse is found,
Far as the curse is found,
Far as, far as, the curse is found.

He rules the world with truth and grace,
And makes the nations prove
The glories of His righteousness,
And wonders of His love,
And wonders of His love,
And wonders, wonders, of His love.

J oy to the World is perhaps the only hymn in this book that is *not* a Christmas carol. Yet, it has been the most published "Christmas hymn" in North America since the 20th century. This enigma may be attributed to non-premillennial interpretations of Watts's hymn that spiritualized his intent. Watts was a premillennialist who loosely based his hymn on Psalm 98, an Enthronement Psalm that describes Christ's Second Coming to rule on earth.

Watts's hymn describes earth receiving her King, men and nature resounding with joy, the curse on earth being removed, and His rule of truth and grace being established over the whole world. However, none of these things came to pass at His First Coming. Psalm 98 has yet to be fulfilled, as does Watts's hymn. We sing this hymn at Christmas in anticipation of His Second Coming.

Will there be a second Christmas commemorating His Second Coming to fulfill Psalm 98 and Watts's hymn? No, Christmas celebrates the birth of the King, but for 1,000 years we will celebrate the annual Feast of Tabernacles. This feast will be a time of rejoicing due to the righteous reign of the Christ and the lifting of the curse on nature. It will truly be a time of "Joy to the world!" At the beginning of the 1,000-year kingdom every heart will have prepared Him room in their life by believing in Him. Heaven and nature will lift their voices in praise because as far as the curse is found His blessings will flow. At last, a King will rule the whole world with truth and grace. The nations will need to prove their devotion to Him by going up annually to worship Him (Zech. 14:16–19). He is worthy of worship.

So, while *Joy to the World* is not a Christmas hymn, it is a hymn that anticipates the King's arrival to reign over the whole world. Because the way into His kingdom at the Second Coming is through the His cross at the First Coming, it is right to sing this amazing hymn at Christmastime. It contains the wonders of His love.

Psalm 98

O sing to the LORD a new song,
For He has done wonderful things,
His right hand and His holy arm
have gained the victory for Him.
The LORD has made known His salvation;
He has revealed His righteousness
in the sight of the nations.
He has remembered His lovingkindness
and His faithfulness to the house of Israel;
All the ends of the earth have seen
the salvation of our God.

Shout joyfully to the LORD, all the earth;
Break forth and sing for joy and sing praises.
Sing praises to the LORD with the lyre,
With the lyre and the sound of melody.
With trumpets and the sound of the horn
Shout joyfully before the King, the LORD.

Let the sea roar and all it contains,
The world and those who dwell in it.
Let the rivers clap their hands,
Let the mountains sing together for joy
Before the LORD,
for He is coming to judge the earth;
He will judge the world with righteousness
And the peoples with equity.

DECEMBER 4

O Come, O Come, Emmanuel

By E Dane Rogers

O Come, O Come, Emmanuel

O come, O come, Emmanuel,
And ransom captive Israel,
That mourns in lonely exile here,
Until the Son of God appear.

Rejoice! Rejoice! Emmanuel
Shall come to thee, O Israel.

O come, Thou Rod of Jesse, free
Thine own from Satan's tyranny;
From depths of hell Thy people save,
And give them victory o'er the grave.

O come, Thou Dayspring, from on high,
And cheer us by Thy drawing nigh;
Disperse the gloomy clouds of night,
And death's dark shadows put to flight.

O come, Thou Key of David, come
And open wide our heav'nly home;
Make safe the way that leads on high,
And close the path to misery.

O come, Adonai, Lord of might,
Who to Thy tribes, on Sinai's height,
In ancient times didst give the law
In cloud and majesty and awe.

O Come, O Come, Emmanuel

W hen I sing this hymn, my mind wanders to memories of Christmas Eve services at my little hometown church—the flicker of candles, the nip of the December air in Washington, and the warmth of the inviting little chapel. These memories go back as far as I can remember, as do most Christmas hymns. But how often do we take a moment to contemplate the words we are singing? And even when we get the gist of the hymn, words like Emmanuel and Dayspring are lost in the fray. Our minds linger for a moment on concepts like Israel's captivity, nations' desire, order and peace, but we forget them as soon as we turn the page in the hymnal and the piano player begins tapping out the next song on the keys.

It is fitting as we celebrate the Advent of the Christ to take pause and consider the words we are singing and the copious biblical revelation and work of God that rests behind many simple lyrics. The words of this song are no different. The promise of their fulfillment goes back to the garden of Eden. When we sing, "O Come, O Come..." We join the heavenly harmony of hopeful saints throughout world history who have longed for the promised Seed of Genesis 3:15, who promised peace and righteousness, the righting of the wrong of sin, and most of all—restoration of broken fellowship with the God who created mankind to enjoy relationship with Him.

But some things are simply lost in translation. The name the hymnist chose to speak of this promised Seed is *Emmanuel*. This is not English. Though most English speakers know the word and know that it speaks of Jesus, the meaning of the name is rich indeed. Scripture itself tells us the meaning of this most significant name.

Matthew 1:23 tells us, "Behold, the virgin shall be with child and shall bear a Son, and they shall call His name Immanuel," which translated means, 'God with us.'" The name *Immanuel* is actually made of three Hebrew words: *im-* meaning "with," *-einu* meaning "us," and *el* meaning "God." Thus, the name Immanuel literally does mean "God (is) with us." This promise of God's presence restored to man is the hope of mankind throughout history, a promise which is amplified to Israel.

The second line of verse one speaks of Israel: "And ransom captive Israel..." The name Immanuel does not original with Matthew; it appears first much earlier on the lips of Isaiah the prophet, who gives King Ahaz a sign of God's faithfulness to Israel, predicting the advent of a child born of a virgin, whose name (the essence of who he is) will be "God with us." Not only was the virgin birth known to Israel (Gen. 3:15, Isa. 7:14), but the deity of the Messiah could also be known if they understood that the promised Seed was Himself to be the presence of God among His people.

It was at the dawn of Israel's captivity in Babylon that this prophetic hope was instilled into the fabric of national Israel. It was under the captivity of Rome, Israel's final captor (Dan. 2) that the Godman was born to the virgin Mary to offer Israel the ultimate guarantee of eternal fellowship and presence with Him—the Messianic kingdom.

Though I am not sure of the hymnist's intentions in placing this verse first in sequence, I like to think it was intentional! Israel did not recognize her Messiah, the Godman born of a virgin, and we non-Jews now share in the hope of Jesus Messiah's second advent, at which time the Day-Star will rise, the gloom of Satan's world system will be shattered, Israel will receive her promised Messiah and Jesus will rule in perfect righteousness — and we will forever be in the presence of God, with perfect holiness and fellowship restored.

Christmas is not just about the incarnation of Christ, or about the redemption he was born to procure. It is about the whole plan and purpose of God concerning His Son. He is the firstborn of creation (Col. 1:15–21) whose human birth secured him the right to inherit the earth. He is coming again, and so we too can rightfully sing in hopeful expectation, "O Come, O Come, Emmanuel, and ransom captive Israel…" The salvation of Israel will be the beginning of the reign of King Jesus.

Matthew 1:20b–23

...behold, an angel of the Lord appeared to him in a dream, saying, "Joseph, son of David, do not be afraid to take Mary as your wife; for the Child who has been conceived in her is of the Holy Spirit. She will bear a Son; and you shall call His name Jesus, for He will save His people from their sins." Now all this took place to fulfill what was spoken by the Lord through the prophet: "Behold, the virgin shall be with child and shall bear a Son, and they shall call His name Immanuel," which translated means, "God with us."

DECEMBER 5

The First Noel

By J. Morgan Arnold

The First Noel

The First Noel the angel did say
Was to certain poor shepherds
in fields as they lay;
In fields as they lay, keeping their sheep,
On a cold winter's night that was so deep.

Noel, Noel, Noel, Noel,
Born is the King of Israel.

They looked up and saw a star
Shining in the east beyond them far,
And to the earth it gave great light,
And so it continued both day and night.

And by the light of that same star
Three wise men came from country far;
To seek for a King was their intent,
And to follow the star wherever it went.

This star drew nigh to the northwest,
O'er Bethlehem it took it rest,
And there it did both stop and stay
Right over the place where Jesus lay.

Then entered in those wise men three
Full reverently upon their knee,
and offered there in His presence
Their gold, and myrrh, and frankincense.

Then let us all with one accord
Sing praises to our heavenly Lord;
That hath made heaven and earth of naught,
And with His blood mankind hath bought.

N oël is not a word commonly employed in our vocabulary today apart from when we sing this song. However, I used it all the time because that was my dad's name! Growing up, my home had many Christmas ornaments and decorations that said "Noel". Christmas was always a special time of year, and he was a special father to us. The word *noël* comes from the French *noel,* meaning *"*Christmas season," which comes from the Old French word *nael,* from the Latin word *natalis* meaning "birth". From *natalis*, we also get the English word "nativity." That little interesting factoid might just help you win a game of Trivial Pursuit one day, or at least impress your friends and family at the next Christmas party!

The First Noël depicts a divine invitation. The most remarkable news of all time was heralded upon the most unremarkable group of people… shepherds. When your job involves personally caring for and protecting smelly animals, you can't help but reek of them. Not only did they immerse themselves in their work, but their "work" immersed itself in them! As a result, many people in Jesus' day were repulsed by shepherds and often viewed them as unskilled or uneducated. But, as we see, that is not the attitude displayed by God or His holy angels. How comforting it is to see and know that God has a soft spot in His heart for those whom society has labeled "the least, the last, and the lost." After all, it brings Him glory that He "has chosen the foolish things of the world to put to shame the wise" (1 Cor. 1:27a).

Once the good news was proclaimed by one angel, the whole night sky became emblazoned with a "multitude of the heavenly host" (Luke 2:13). At this point, these shepherds had a choice to make. They could either get up, go into town and search for this Messianic Babe or remain sitting around the campfire and just chalk up their vision to a case of undercooked mutton. Thankfully, they chose option one. How amazing to think that after all the baby lambs they had witnessed being birthed on their watch, they would be the first ones to see the Lamb of God after He was born.

Then God used a special star to "call" wise men from the East to come and see this special Child (Matt. 2:1–2). One fact that can easily get lost in this story is that these men were not ethnic Jews; they were Gentiles. So, not only did God send the divine birth announcement out to a group of lowly shepherds, but He also invited truth-seeking non-Jews to come and worship the King of the Jews.

In the opening chapters of the New Testament an angelic call beckoned people to come to Christ. In bookend fashion, we also see a divine call for all to come to Christ in the last chapter of the Bible (Rev. 22:17). Let's not forget that the Babe who was marveled at in the manger will one day be marveled at by His Bride, the Church, whom He will meet in the clouds (1 Thess. 4:17). It is this newborn Babe who will return as the King of Kings to establish His Kingdom.

Until then, God in His infinite grace cordially keeps the door open, inviting anyone with ears to hear and heed the Gospel, anyone who is blind and desires to see, anyone who is parched with a thirst that no libation on earth can quench (not even eggnog or hot apple cider), to come and believe in Jesus for eternal life. If you've already tasted of His living water, you can testify of its life-giving qualities. But, if you haven't yet, you are invited. The shepherds came. The magi came. Now, it's your turn. Jesus said, "whoever drinks of the water that I shall give him will never thirst... it will become in him a fountain of water springing up into everlasting life" (John 4:14). Come drink the water that only Christ can give. He offers it freely to you. After all, He paid for it with His own blood.

Revelation 22:17

And the Spirit and the bride say, "Come!" And let him who hears say, "Come!" And let him who thirsts come. Whoever desires, let him take the water of life freely.

DECEMBER 6

Ukrainian Christmas Carol

By Paul Miles

Good Evening to You

Ukrainian Christmas Carol:
Dobryi Vechir Tobi

Good evening to you, Mr. *Hospodar*

Rejoice!
Oh world rejoice,
The Son of God is born!

Cover the table
And everything with *kylymy*,

And put out *kalachi*
Made from spring wheat.

For three holidays are coming
To you as guests:

And the first holiday is Christmas,

And the second holiday is St. Basil's Day,

And the third holiday is Theophany.

I n the Ukrainian tradition, there are several winter Christian holidays. The song *Dobryi Vechir Tobi* is more than a celebration of Christmas; it is a celebration of three holidays.

Ukraine has an ancient pre-Christian tradition of *koliadkas*, or carols that would be sung from house to house. *Dobryi Vechir Tobi* is a *koliadka* that is set in front of a home. It is directed to the head of the house (Ukr. *hospodar*) and the singers tell him to set up his home with *kylymy*, which are decorative rugs and *kalachi*, which are round woven breads.

Then the singers announce that three holidays are coming: Christmas on December 25th, St. Basil's Day on January 1st, and Theophany on January 6th.

Longer versions of the song go on to say that these three holidays will bring comfort, happiness, and fortune to all of Ukraine (perhaps some of the pre-Christian roots are showing through there). The Christian is under no command to celebrate any holidays, though he is free to do so (Col. 1:16–17) and I think we could benefit from celebrating these holidays if we do so under freedom rather than obligation.

The first holiday is Christmas, the celebration of the birth of Christ, when the Word had become Flesh and was birthed by a virgin. You already know about that one. The second holiday is St. Basil's Day. Basil of Caesarea was a 4th-century

Greek bishop who defended the doctrine of Christ from the heresies of Arianism (which denied Christ's deity) and Apollinarism (which diminished Christ's humanity). The third holiday is Theophany. This is a holiday that commemorates the baptism of Jesus. One way to celebrate Theophany is to go to the Dnipro River or another body of water, cut a hole in the ice, and jump in.

This Christmas season, I would challenge you to think about more than the event of Christ's birth (as significant as that is). Think about how the nativity relates to everything that follows in the life of Christ as well as how we must continue to stand for the biblical doctrines of Christ's deity today.

In fact, why not start today? This is St. Nicholas' Day, December 6th, which has nothing to do with that fake punk, Santa Claus. The real St. Nicholas was a theologian who participated in the Council of Nicaea, and, according to legend, smacked Arius the heretic. You can celebrate by giving candy to your children and reminding them about the deity of Christ.

Psalm 106:5

"That I may see the benefit of Your chosen ones, That I may rejoice in the gladness of Your nation, That I may glory with Your inheritance."

DECEMBER 7

God Rest Ye Merry Gentlemen

By Jacob Heaton

God Rest Ye Merry Gentlemen

God rest you merry, gentlemen,
Let nothing you dismay,
Remember Christ our Savior
Was born on Christmas Day
To save us all from Satan's pow'r
When we were gone astray.

O tidings of comfort and joy,
comfort and joy;
O tidings of comfort and joy.

From God our heav'nly Father
A blessed angel came
And unto certain shepherds
Brought tidings of the same;
How that in Bethlehem was born
The Son of God by name.

Now to the Lord sing praises
All you within this place,
And with true love and brotherhood
Each other new embrace;
This holy tide of Christmas
All other doth deface.

God Rest Ye Merry Gentlemen

T he context of *God Rest Ye Merry Gentlemen* is important and further magnifies the already powerful words of the song. While the first and last stanzas direct the broad audience of Christians in every age to rest in the wonderful news that the Savior has been born, the middle three stanzas establish the context for the meaning of the song. This shepherd narrative is quite familiar, but I think the circumstance of these herdsmen make the good news even greater. There are four things worth considering this Christmas season.

The shepherds were Israelites. As such they are God's chosen people and recipients of important promises that God has declared to them. This detail captures the reality that all the promises made in the Hebrew Scriptures concerning the future expectations of the Jewish people have not been realized. The good news these Shepherds heard alludes to the fact that God is now moving towards bringing their hope to fruition.

The Israelites at this time were under Roman occupation. God promised the Israelites land, seed, and blessing. These promises are later specified to include a king from the Davidic line that would rule and reign forever. The news of this baby boy signals that this very king has been born. This certainly is cause for celebration and a call for Israel to consider their covenant with God.

The shepherds were likely Levitical shepherds charged with caring for the lambs that would later be used for the sacrifices on behalf of the nation. Not many would be excited that they would soon be laid off, but the news of the Messiah's birth foreshadows that He is the One to deliver them from their sins and bring about their promised kingdom.

Many commentaries make mention of the historical understanding that in Medieval times "merry" meant "mighty" and "rest" meant "to keep", or "to make". This would make the medieval lyrics: "God make ye mighty gentlemen." A comparison to this medieval understanding is that Robin Hood's "merry men" were in fact "mighty men." While it is difficult to find primary source evidence to confirm this linguistic development, if true, the modification changes the meaning slightly and certainly imbues the sentiment the angels communicated to the shepherds in the declaration "fear not" (Luke 2:10).

Isaiah 40:1

""Comfort, yes, comfort My people!" Says your God."

DECEMBER 8

O Come, All Ye Faithful

By Tom Stegall

O Come, All Ye Faithful

O come, all ye faithful,
joyful and triumphant.
O come ye, O come ye to Bethlehem.
Come and behold Him
—born the King of angels!

O come, let us adore Him!
O come, let us adore Him!
O come, let us adore Him
—Christ, the Lord!

Sing, choirs of angels;
sing in exultation.
O sing, all ye bright hosts
of heav'n above.
Glory to God, all glory in the highest!

Yea, Lord, we greet Thee,
born this happy morning.
O Jesus, to Thee be all glory giv'n:
Word of the Father,
now in flesh appearing!

E veryone loves newborn babies. I distinctly
remember the birth of my firstborn. There
in the hospital delivery room, the
obstetrician turned to me at that moment and asked
if I wished to cut the umbilical cord, just as he had
routinely done countless times with other fathers.
But I just stared back at him blankly like a deer in
the headlights and then silently shook my head
sideways to indicate "no." I was speechless and
mesmerized at the birth of my son. It literally took
my breath away. From that moment on, my wife
and I adored our precious new gift from God.

How often have we heard these words uttered
over a baby: "He's so adorable"? Of course, this is
usually spoken in the context of the baby's cuteness.
But these words were never more fitting than as the
response of appropriate, genuine worship at the
birth of the Worthy One (Rev. 5:9). The title of this
Christmas song, *O Come, All Ye Faithful*, is taken
from the first words of its first verse. But the
emphasis of the song is not on the faithfulness of the
worshiper but on the greatness of the One
worshiped, the Lord Jesus Christ. Thus, three times
the refrain repeats "O Come, let us adore Him."

He and He alone is worthy to be worshiped. It
is to Him we are invited as believers to come in
humble adoration. The song also declares, "O Jesus,
to Thee be all glory giv'n." This parallels Luke 2:32
where the infant Jesus is called "the glory of Your
people Israel." Why is Jesus elsewhere called "the

Lord of glory" (1 Cor. 2:8) and thus deserving of all glory and worship? Because of who He inherently is and what He has done for us.

No doubt, Joseph and Mary's baby was not the first that Simeon ever held in his arms. He had waited his whole life to see and to hold this particular baby. This baby boy was none other than "the Lord's Christ" (Luke 2:26), the Messiah promised by God to Israel. Thus, at the end of each refrain we proclaim that He truly is "Christ, the Lord." As the "Word of the Father, now in flesh appearing," Jesus became the incarnate revelation of God to man (John 1:1, 14). He became "a light to bring revelation to the Gentiles" (Luke 2:32), that we may know the Father (John 14:7–9) and have a relationship with Him through this Light (John 1:9; 9:5).

This "King of angels," so majestic in glory, humbled Himself to such an extent (Phil. 2:5–8) that He went to the Cross to die for our sins in full. Thus, He came to us not only with light to reveal God but with "salvation" (Luke 2:30) as a gift from God to save us from our sins (Matt. 1:21). What should be our response as believers and recipients? O come, all ye faithful; O come, let us adore Him, Christ, the Lord!

Revelation 5:9-10

And they sang a new song, saying: "You are worthy to take the scroll, And to open its seals; For You were slain, And have redeemed us to God by Your blood Out of every tribe and tongue and people and nation, And have made us kings and priests to our God; And we shall reign on the earth."

DECEMBER 9

Angels, From the Realms of Glory

By Luther Smith

Angels, From the Realms of Glory

Angels from the realms of glory,
wing your flight o'er all the earth;
ye who sang creation's story,
now proclaim Messiah's birth.

Come and worship, come and worship;
worship Christ, the newborn King.

Shepherds in the field abiding,
watching o'er your flocks by night:
God with us is now residing;
yonder shines the infant Light.

Sages, leave your contemplations;
brighter visions beam afar;
seek the great desire of nations;
ye have seen his natal star.

Saints, before the altar bending,
watching long in hope and fear,
suddenly the Lord, descending,
in his temple shall appear.

Though an infant now we view him,
he shall fill his Father's throne,
gather all the nations to him;
every knee shall then bow down.

C hristmas is one of the best times of the year, not just for the Christmas lights, trees, hot chocolate, and holiday trappings that make this time of year so special but also for the hymns that compel a person to contemplate and reflect on the incredible birth of Jesus Christ. This short hymn covers so many aspects of our Savior. The writer of this Christmas hymn centers our attention in each verse on a particular group and the part they play in honoring this divine infant.

Let us begin with the first group: the angels. Angels were there to witness creation itself being made (Job 38:7). The hymn tells the angels "who sang creation's story" now proclaim "Messiah's birth." This is a beautiful verse because it reminds the singer that the God, who made the heavens and the earth *and the angels*, acknowledged the Messiah, His Anointed.

The second group is the shepherds: men of low and humble estate who work and watch over their flocks in the evening. This connects the first and second verses in this hymn as in the historical account in the Gospel of Luke. The angels come to the shepherds by night and tell them of the Child who had been born (Luke 2:8–14). What is the importance of all this fanfare and spectacle? The hymn answers this question. "God with us is now residing!" Ahhh! That is who this Child is! God in human flesh who became like His creation and dwelt among His creation! What a truth to contemplate!

The third group is the sages, who are wise and ponder deep things. Yet the hymn tells the "wise men" to leave their thoughts and seek "brighter visions [that] beam afar." The title "Messiah" is a Hebrew term that all Hebrews would have recognized. However, the hymn mentions the Messiah is not limited to the nation of Israel but that He is "the great desire of nations" who have observed, "His natal star" (Matt. 2:1–10). Such a verse calls to mind the magi and their journey to pay homage and honor this babe with their kingly gifts—frankincense, gold, and myrrh.

The fourth group in this hymn throughout the ages that have dedicated their lives to Christ (notice the mention of the altar in this verse) and their eager expectation and prayer to see the Lord descending in His temple. Unlike the previous verse, this is not a glimpse into the past, but the *future*. The hope of all saints, especially those who are persecuted or martyred, is that this babe, who bears the title of Messiah, who is God incarnate, will rule and reign in the future (Rev. 19:11–19). This is no ordinary baby. This is our Savior, our Hero, the Righteous One who will rule with these saints forever. What a promise found in the verse of this song!

The fifth and final group in this hymn is *us*. The hymn draws the singer's attention to the present, and *we* are told to focus *our* gaze and reflect on this infant and His destiny. He will take His rightful place and rule on the throne on behalf of His Father.

All nations will recognize Him for who He is and honor him by bowing down to him. Such a promise is also found in the Scriptures (Phil. 2:9–11).

And we *cannot* forget the refrain. Every time the refrain is sung, it gives the participant all aspects: Past, present, and future in two simple lines: Come and worship, come and worship *(present)*, worship Christ the newborn *(past)* King *(future)*.

What a wonderful hymn to move our minds to think about not just the first advent of Messiah (which we celebrate) but also the second advent (which we anticipate) and all the involved groups. As you sing this hymn, may you be in a state of thankfulness and hope like the saints, recognize like the shepherds, seek like the sages, and proclaim like the angels that our God, who was *the* infant, will be acknowledged as *the* King. Amen.

Soli Deo Gloria!

2 Peter 1:19 & Revelation 22:16

So we have the prophetic word made more sure, to which you do well to pay attention as to a lamp shining in a dark place, until the day dawns and the morning star arises in your hearts…

"I, Jesus, have sent My angel to testify to you these things for the churches. I am the root and the descendant of David, the bright morning star."

DECEMBER 10

O Holy Night

By Matt Fehrn

O Holy Night

O holy night! The stars are brightly shining;
It is the night of the dear Savior's birth.
Long lay the world in sin and error pining,
Till He appeared, and the soul felt its worth.
A thrill of hope—the weary world rejoices,
For yonder breaks a new and glorious morn!

Fall on your knees!
O hear the angel voices!
O night divine, O night when Christ was born!
O night, O holy night, O night divine!

Led by the light of faith serenely beaming,
With glowing hearts by His cradle we stand.
So led by light of a star sweetly gleaming,
Here came the Wise Men from Orient land.
The King of kings lay thus in lowly manger,
In all our trials born to be our Friend.
He knows our need—to our weakness is no stranger.
Behold your King, before Him lowly bend! (x2)

Truly He taught us to love one another;
His law is love and His gospel is peace.
Chains shall He break, for the slave is our brother,
And in His name all oppression shall cease.
Sweet hymns of joy in grateful chorus raise we;
Let all within us praise His holy name.
Christ is the Lord! O praise His name forever!
His pow'r and glory evermore proclaim! (x2)

T he story goes that this hymn was first a poem written in 1847 in France by a man named Placide Cappeau. He wrote it while thinking about the birth of Jesus. Then he went to a friend, Adolphe Charles Adams, a classical musician who composed the music for the poem. "Cantique de Noel" was performed at a midnight mass shortly thereafter on Christmas Eve.

Several years later, John Sullivan Dwight translated the song into English and called it "O Holy Night." He was an abolitionist who was persuaded by the song's third verse:

> "Truly He taught us to love one another;
> His law is love and His gospel is peace.
> Chains shall He break for the slave is our brother,
> And in His name all oppression shall cease."

The song then became popular in the United States. On Christmas Eve in 1906, Reginald Fessenden, a radio pioneer, broadcast the first ever musical program over the airwaves. The song he broadcast was "O Holy Night."

As sinful human beings, we never fully appreciate much of the grace that has been bestowed on us. None of us knows what it is like to live in a world where our Lord and Savior, Jesus Christ, did not exist. I want to take you back 2,000 years to the town of Bethlehem. Imagine growing up as a Jew. They were under the oppression of the Romans, waiting for hundreds of years for the promised

Messiah while Judaism was being perverted by legalistic religious leaders.

Then came a glorious answer to their prayers! Jesus Christ, the promised Messiah, was born. Think of the words, "Fall on your knees, O hear the angel voices, O night divine". Through these words we can extrapolate the only proper response to the most gracious gift God bestowed on all mankind—the gift of God the Father, sending His Son to earth as a man to die on the cross to pay for the sins of the world. Think of the angels as they watched the Lord of Lords descend into this cesspool that we call earth to subjugate himself to every evil deed, thought, or action that man has ever committed.

The sheer thought of the greatest act of love and sacrifice that has ever occurred in the heavens or the earth should cause us to fall on our knees and thank Him, every minute of every day. It should cause us to think about God's perfect plan that would solve the problem of sin which man had brought upon himself. We do not earn or deserve it, but because of His marvelous grace, God chose to perform this action. He did it because He knew that it was the only way that all who choose to believe in Jesus Christ could have eternal life.

This Christmas season, let us approach every moment with the proper reverence and thankfulness that is demanded by our Lord's matchless and perfect grace gift of salvation. Let us also remember that Christ's earthly ministry is only part of the plan.

He still lives! He will return to earth once more, as Lord of Lords, and King of Kings. As believers, we will return with Him. After His Millennial reign is over, we get to spend eternity with Him praising His name forever! O Holy Night indeed.

John 14:18-19

"I will not leave you as orphans; I will come to you. After a little while the world will no longer see Me, but you will see Me; because I live, you will live also.

DECEMBER 11

It Came Upon the Midnight Clear

By Dr. Mark Mills

It Came Upon the Midnight Clear

It came upon the midnight clear,
That glorious song of old,
From angels bending near the earth
To touch their harps of gold;
"Peace on the earth, good will to men
From heaven's all-gracious King" –
The world in solemn stillness lay
To hear the angels sing.

Still through the cloven skies they come
With peaceful wings unfurled,
And still their heavenly music floats
O'er all the weary world;
Above its sad and lowly plains
They bend on hovering wing,
And ever o'er its Babel-sounds
The blessed angels sing.

And ye, beneath life's crushing load,
Whose forms are bending low,
Who toil along the climbing way
With painful steps and slow,
Look now! for glad and golden hours
Come swiftly on the wing; –
Oh, rest beside the weary road
And hear the angels sing!

For lo! the days are hastening on
By prophet bards foretold,
When with the ever circling years
Comes round the age of gold;
When Peace shall over all the earth
Its ancient splendors fling,
And the whole world give back the song
Which now the angels sing.

P oetry set to music dresses its message in clothing that captivates not only the mind but the heart, both the thoughts and emotions of the singer and hearer. It's no wonder the profound events of Christmas have been rehearsed for generations through carols like this one, adorning the birth of the Savior with enduring images. This song paints backdrops, arranges the stage, and clothes the various actors to bring a story from long ago to life in the present. The beauty of the angelic hosts as they come to the lowly shepherds in Luke 2:8–14 offers a series of strong contrasts between the ideal and the mundane.

The first scene opens with the stage set in the dark of night. The darkness is dispelled by the glorious appearing of the angels, as Luke writes that "the glory of the Lord shone round about" the shepherds. These angels come near the earth with a message for mankind of peace and good will from the gracious King of heaven. The audience sees an image of angels with golden harps singing the wonderful message to a world quietly lying in their solemn, joyless night. The splendor of the messengers with their melodious words of grace from heaven is heightened by the contrasting darkness, quietness, and solemn state of people on the earth.

For the next scene the stage depicting the shepherds' field is transformed to reveal the earth eighteen hundred years later. One might expect the heavenly messengers to have had a powerful impact on the state of mankind, even as the glorious song and its message of peace and good will is present on stage, continuing to ring out through time. Yet the world remains in weariness, sadness, and confusion. From the skies above the lowly plains, the music of harmonious, angelic singing is still heard over the discordant sounds rising from the earth.

The stage lights now turn toward the audience, revealing a dismal picture as they play a part in this production. People moving along the road of life under tremendous weight, slowly, painfully working their way up a steep incline. Now a call invites them to pause, rest, and listen to the song of the angels, because there is hope for joy that is coming "on the wing," just as the angels came to the shepherds long ago. Burdens, pain, and toil will give way to "glad and golden hours."

Back on the stage, the final scene is illuminated, exposing a panorama of golden brightness, the consummation of prophetic expectation. With all the earth in view, peace adorns every vista, and perfect harmony between earth and heaven reigns. No contrasts can be seen here, only perfect peace in a world that experiences and embodies the gracious message of heaven's King.

The carol mentions ancient prophets foretelling a golden age, which can best be summarized by one of the most-quoted Old Testament passages at Christmastime, Isaiah 9:6–7.

Jesus Christ is the child that was born, the Son of God who was given, the central figure of the Christmas story.

The next time you hear or sing *It Came upon the Midnight Clear*, think of history as God's script, the world as the stage, and every angelic and human being as participants playing out our roles under his direction. God the Father cast his Son in the role of the Prince of Peace, wearing the crown and finery that fits his character, who will rule the earth in an unending reign of peace. Let this carol's rich images and contrasts fill your mind and draw your heart to this Savior King. Only in him can we find peace with God and other people, and have hope for a glorious future, freed from the darkness of this life into the splendor of eternal peace.

Isaiah 9:6–7

For unto us a child is born, unto us a son is given: And the government shall be upon his shoulder: And his name shall be called Wonderful, Counselor, The mighty God, The everlasting Father, The Prince of Peace. Of the increase of his government and peace there shall be no end, Upon the throne of David, and upon his kingdom, To order it, and to establish it with judgment and with justice from henceforth even forever. The zeal of the LORD of hosts will perform this.

DECEMBER 12

Little Drummer Boy

By J. Morgan Arnold

Little Drummer Boy

Come they told me,
A new born King to see,
Our finest gifts we bring,
To lay before the King,

So to honor Him,
When we come.

Little Baby,
I am a poor boy too,
I have no gift to bring,
That's fit to give the King,

Shall I play for you,
On my drum?

Mary nodded,
The ox and lamb kept time,
I played my drum for Him,
Then He smiled at me,
Me and my drum.

T he song and story of *The Little Drummer Boy* were favorites of mine growing up. I fondly remember the 25-minute 1968 Claymation special that was shown on network TV every Christmas season.

The central character is a young boy named Aaron who was given a drum by his father. He cherished the drum and its beat even made some of the farm animals dance when he played. However, his happiness was stolen from him one night and replaced with hatred for all people after robbers killed his father and burned down the farm. Only Aaron, a camel, a donkey, and a sheep escaped. Circumstances brought these characters into contact with a caravan of three kings who were following a bright star in the sky.

The kings had need of another camel, so they paid Aaron's handler, a unscrupulous showman, a large sum of money for Aaron's camel against his wishes. After the caravan left, Aaron abandoned his handler in search of his camel. Remembering how the kings mentioned they were going to a place where the star led them, he, too, looked up into the sky and followed the star to the town of Bethlehem.

He noticed scores of shepherds walking to a stable that had a glowing light emanating from it. There, he was reunited with his camel and the kings, but even more amazing to him was the little baby in the manger. Knowing that he was too poor to offer a costly gift, he offered to play a song on his drum for the baby and His parents. Mary agreed to it. At the end of his song, he looked up and saw Baby Jesus smiling at him. As a result, Aaron's happiness returned as he realized that this was no ordinary child, He was much more.

This story does not exactly follow the biblical narrative. Some artistic license was taken in various parts of the story for it to come together as it does. However, I do believe there are a couple of nuggets of biblical truth that can be derived from the story and song as we ponder it.

None of us who come to Jesus, understanding that we need a Savior, has any gift, possession, or personal qualities that would be worthy to purchase our salvation. Isaiah 64:6a states, "But we are all like an unclean thing, and all our righteousness is like filthy rags." Romans 3:23 agrees: "…for all have sinned and fall short of the glory of God."

The richest man in the world cannot buy a ticket to heaven. The smartest person in the world with the highest IQ is not able to produce a mathematical equation to solve the problem of sin. The best team of scientists on the planet is not able to develop a special elixir to grant eternal life. The strongest man in the world, let alone the strongest army in the world, cannot bust down the gates of heaven. In fact, if the sum total of all human ingenuity in the world, all human wisdom, all human education, all human talents and abilities, and all human compassion and benevolence could all be tallied together, it would still fall short of what is required for righteous before a holy God.

Thankfully, God does not require us to bring our gifts to Him for salvation. Instead, He requires us to receive *His* gift—the free gift of salvation purchased by Jesus for you and for me on a Roman cross on Mount Calvary. His death, burial, and resurrection from the dead have granted a full pardon from sin and a guaranteed promise of eternal life to all who no more than believe in the person and work of Jesus Christ. Ephesians 2:8–9 reads, "For by grace you have been saved through faith, and that not of yourselves; it is the gift of God, *not of works*, lest anyone should boast."

Not only has God graciously saved us, but He has also equipped us for service. Ephesians 2:10 says, "For we are His workmanship, created in Christ Jesus for good works, which God prepared beforehand that we should walk in them." The works we do for God are not to maintain our salvation or merit some special favors from Him. We simply serve Jesus with our gifts and talents as a way to say "Thank You" to Him. If you are a teacher, teach your best for Him. If you are a handyman, fix and repair things as best you can for Him. And… if you are a drummer, play your best for Him. He will smile at you… you and your little drum.

1 Corinthians 12:4–7

"There are diversities of gifts, but the same Spirit. There are differences of ministries, but the same Lord. And there are diversities of activities, but it is the same God who works all in all. But the manifestation of the Spirit is given to each one for the profit *of all.*"

Colossians 3:15–17

"And let the peace of God rule in your hearts, to which also you were called in one body; and be thankful. Let the word of Christ dwell in you richly in all wisdom, teaching and admonishing one another in psalms and hymns and spiritual songs, singing with grace in your hearts to the Lord. And *whatever* you do in word or deed, *do* all in the name of the Lord Jesus, giving thanks to God the Father through Him."

DECEMBER 13

Go Tell It on the Mountain

By Eric Plemel

Go Tell It on the Mountain

Go, tell it on the mountain,
over the hills, and ev'rywhere;
go, tell it on the mountain
that Jesus Christ is born.

While shepherds kept their watching
o'er silent flocks by night,
behold, throughout the heavens
there shone a holy light.

The shepherds feared and trembled
when lo, above the earth
rang out the angel chorus
that hailed our Savior's birth.

Down in a lowly manger
the humble Christ was born,
and God sent us salvation
that blessed Christmas morn.

Go Tell It on the Mountain

I love a good Christmas carol worship service and I love singing Christmas songs around a living room piano. I would host a Christmas music sing-along every month if I could get enough participation! There is something special about singing with a group of believers, and there is something especially happy about Christmas music. If I were planning a sing-along, this song would be the conclusion every time. However, the happy refrain does not urge us to stay inside and tell it to the Christians.

Hearing the story of Christmas is, no doubt, of great spiritual benefit to Christians. Pastors and the Sunday school teachers should be reminded frequently too. But this song causes us to lift our eyes and see abroad. It urges us to lift our voice and tell it everywhere—outside your home, outside your church.

To begin telling the whole creation, God sent angels to deliver the "glad tidings… to all people" (Luke 2:10). Yet, God's wonderful wisdom only delivered the news to a handful of individuals. The shepherds heard, came to see that it was true, and then they immediately spread the word (Luke 2:17). Nobody told them to tell it on the mountain—they couldn't help themselves! And beginning with the shepherds, God's plan to tell the world was set into action. Believers began to tell it: "Jesus Christ is born."

Another early adopter of God's "Go, Tell It" plan was an old woman named Anna (Luke 2:36–38). She lived in Jerusalem, and when she saw the newborn king visiting the temple with Mary and Joseph, she was beyond excited. And what did Anna's excitement compel her to do? She told the news all around town.

It is easy to think, *nobody really wants to hear about Jesus, so I won't bother telling them*, but the shepherds didn't care. They told everyone they saw. Anna, on the other hand, "spoke of Him to all those who looked for redemption in Jerusalem" (Luke 2:38). This means she went to the trouble to find out who wanted to hear about a Redeemer. Imagine the conversations she must have had!

Go tell the news to that friend. Invite that co-worker to church. Ask questions to find out if that family member cares about heaven or sin or redemption. Every generation has included a majority that is independent of God. Every generation has also included a minority that is soft toward God. Go, tell it. You might be surprised who wants to hear.

Mark 16:15

And He said to them, "Go into all the world and preach the gospel to every creature."

DECEMBER 14

For Unto Us a Child Is Born

By David Roseland

For Unto Us a Child Is Born

For unto us a Child is born,
unto us a Son is given,
and the government shall be
upon His shoulder;
and his name shall be called
Wonderful Counsellor,
the Mighty God,
the Everlasting Father,
the Prince of Peace

(Isaiah 9:6)

For Unto Us a Child Is Born

T here is perhaps no better Christmas carol to
bring the Messianic Hope of Israel into
focus at Christmastime than this little tune
tucked away into track 8 (Movement 12) of Handel's
Messiah. Many today have probably not heard this
Christmas carol, except classical music buffs. That
was true for me until about twelve years ago, and
then one early December morning I heard my new
favorite carol of all time.

God providentially surprised me with one of
those amazing, beautiful, rare moments we tend to
remember for life. It was dark, it was cold, and I was
on time—but just barely. I was in a hurry on the way
to the Boston airport around 4:30 AM to catch an
early flight for a Bible conference and I had the
interstate to myself. I popped Handel's *Messiah* into
my car's CD player and turned the volume up way
too loud. I had only ever heard the "Hallelujah"
chorus. I was overdue listening to the entire oratorio.

It had been all very pleasant and interesting, and
then the sopranos started with their light introduction
to the melody of "For Unto Us a Child is Born." It is
such a pretty tune, and it stood out right away from
the rest of the work. I thought, "that's a perfect
setting to the words of Isaiah 9:6." This is a sweet,
delightful thing with these wonderful, gentle voices
singing "for unto us a Child is born, a Son is
given…" Then the men and women started singing
this theme back-and-forth as they always must in
these classical oratorios. It was so well-balanced,

though, and I thought, "that is really nice." Ni-hi-hi-hi-hi-hi-hi-hice.

But then Handel absolutely devastated me with what he and the orchestra did to Isaiah 9:6b. The contrapuntal celebration of verse 6a was building to the union of all parts in majestic harmony together, blasting out, "WONDERFUL! COUNSELOR! THE MIGHTY GOD! THE EVERLASTING FATHER! THE PRINCE OF PEACE!" I wish you could have been there.

This work of classical music really wants a full chorus and orchestra, and I think it is a rare example of human music that fits divine subject matter. There is no more majestic proclamation in all human history than the hope of Israel announced through the 8th Century BC Prince of prophets, Isaiah.

The coming Messiah will be born to Israel, and He will be the Son of God. His birth is promised in the same breath as His eternal rule! He will bring the promised Kingdom of God on earth. The Person of Christmas will be God—"Mighty God," yet born in the flesh of man—"Unto us a Child will be born." He would not be God the Father, of course, but the Son of God, Who as Creator and eternal King of kings is the "Father of Eternity."

If you dig a little into the Hebrew here, "Wonderful counselor" is probably better rendered "marvelous planner or strategist." Often this word is used of military planning. Isaiah's "names" for the

Son in 9:6 begin with military overtones and end with the desired outcome of all warfare, for He will forever be "the Prince of Peace."

Verse 7 describes the coming, promised, eternal Kingdom of God. When the Lord Jesus Christ sets up His Kingdom, Isaiah tells us that its glory will be ever-*expanding*. There will be no end to the *increase* of His government. There will be no end of His peace! The Child will be an Israelite King on David's Throne in Jerusalem, and from that Jewish throne He will rule the world. The Christmas Child will fulfill the Davidic Covenant of 2 Samuel 7. Jesus, God the Son, will establish this Kingdom in righteousness and justice, and it will never cease. All by God's great zeal for His glory.

We, the Church, the Body of Christ, will accompany our Bridegroom in the establishment of this Kingdom. We will be the "children of God" in Romans 8 who will marvel and witness the beginning of this mighty work, and verse 21 says we somehow will participate in the liberation of the world from its curse and corruption. The lowly shepherds surrounded by myriads of the heavenly host demonstrate the great contrast between our Savior's lowly birth and His glorious destiny. Christmas in Isaiah 9 means the Kingdom is *coming*!

Psalm 2:6–8

"But as for Me, I have installed My King
Upon Zion, My holy mountain."
"I will surely tell of the decree of the LORD:
He said to Me, 'You are My Son,
Today I have begotten You.
'Ask of Me, and I will surely give the nations as Your
    inheritance,
And the *very* ends of the earth as Your possession.

DECEMBER 15

Hark! The Herald Angels Sing

By Dr. Robert L. Dean

Hark! The Herald Angels Sing

Hark! the herald angels sing,
"Glory to the new-born King;
peace on earth, and mercy mild—
God and sinners reconciled!"
Joyful, all ye nations rise,
join the triumph of the skies;
with th' angelic hosts proclaim,
"Christ is born in Bethlehem!"
Hark the herald angels sing,
"Glory to the new-born King!"

Christ, by highest heav'n adored,
Christ, the everlasting Lord!
Late in time behold Him come,
offspring of the virgin's womb.
Veiled in flesh the God-head see;
hail th' incarnate Deity,
pleased as man with men to dwell,
Jesus, our Emmanuel.
Hark! the herald angels sing,
"Glory to the new-born King."

Hail the heav'n-born Prince of Peace!
Hail the Sun of Righteousness!
Light and life to all He brings,
ris'n with healing in His wings.
Mild He lays His glory by,
born that man no more may die,
born to raise the sons of earth,
born to give them second birth.
Hark! the herald angels sing,
"Glory to the new-born King."

O
ne dark night over 2,000 years ago,
shepherds were in their field watching
over a unique flock of sheep. These were
special shepherds, Levitical priests, watching over
the Temple flock that provided the sheep for
sacrifices. Suddenly the heavens exploded in light
as an angel appeared to make the announcement of
the ages. Christ, *Yeshua*, the promised and
prophesied *Moshiach* of Israel was born.

The angelic proclamation of the birth of
Yeshua, the *Moshiach* of Israel has inspired several
hymns. This one by Charles Wesley, and later set to
music written by Felix Mendelssohn, is a Christmas
favorite that is rich with doctrine.

Charles Wesley (1707–1788) is often said to
have been "the greatest hymnwriter of the ages." He
along with his older brother, John (1703–1791), and
evangelist George Whitefield (1714–1770) laid the
foundation for the reform movement in the
Anglican Church later known as Methodism.
Charles wrote just under 9,000 hymns. Among these
hymns are numerous others which continue to be
sung today: *And Can It Be*, *O for a Thousand
Tongues to Sing*, *Christ the Lord is Risen Today*, to
name a few. *Hark! The Herald Angels Sing*, has
become a favorite Christmas hymn for many.

This was one of few Christmas songs written in
the 17th and 18th centuries. From the time of the
ascendancy of the Puritans in the early 1600's,
Christmas hymns had been outlawed. Puritans

frowned upon the excesses that had come to characterize Christmas celebrations. But Wesley presents the clear biblical truth of the birth of Jesus the Messiah (Anointed One) to be the future King of Israel and the ruler of the world.

Jesus entered the world according to biblical prophecy, a direct descendant of King David not through his son Solomon, but through his son Nathan, avoiding the cursed line Jeconiah. Wesley clearly articulates that the expectation of the coming Messiah would bring peace upon the earth, under His future rule.

The first verse opens with a majestic call to focus on the announcement of the angels. Our minds are elevated to the vaults of heaven. In fact, Wesley's original first line called attention to this, "Hark! how all the *welkin* (archaic for the vault of heaven)—rings. We are grateful to the renowned evangelist of the Great Awakening, George Whitefield, for altering that line to the present, "Hark, the herald angels sing." The majesty of the melody fits the cry and draws our attention to the heavens still, focusing on that wonderful message.

The first verse centers our attention on that long-expected proclamation as the first stanza recalls the announcement of the Savior's birth and tightly connects it to His initial purpose at His coming—to offer to Israel their promised kingdom and king. Christ is extolled as King, then reconciler, and the focus for the worshipper is on the birth of the unique One of all history.

The second stanza begins and ends with reference to Isaiah 7:14. First, we recall the virgin conception and birth (Isa. 7:14), combined with an allusion to that glorious explanation of the incarnation of the eternal Second Person of the Trinity adding true, unfallen humanity to His now veiled Deity. Second, Wesley deftly combines this biblical truth with the Hebrew title, Immanuel, "God with us."

In the third stanza our gaze is first shifted to the prophet Malachi, who speaks of the Prince of Peace (Isa. 9:6) as the Sun of Righteousness who will bring "healing in His wings." (Mal. 4:2). Then Wesley brings us again to the humility of the Son who veiled His glory that He might provide regeneration to the spiritual dead of the earthy. For all of that we surely should sing, "Glory, to the newborn King."

Isaiah 7:14

"Therefore the Lord Himself will give you a sign: Behold, the virgin shall conceive and bear a Son, and shall call His name Immanuel."

DECEMBER 16

I Heard the Bells on Christmas Day

By Kurt Witzig

I Heard the Bells on Christmas Day

I heard the bells on Christmas day
Their old familiar carols play,
And wild and sweet the words repeat
Of peace of earth, good will to men.

I thought how, as the day had come,
The belfries of all Christendom
Had rolled along th'unbroken song
Of peace on earth, good will to men.

And in despair I bowed my head:
"There is no peace on earth," I said,
"For hate is strong, and mocks the song
Of peace on earth, good will to men."

Then pealed the bells more loud and deep:
"God is not dead, nor doth He sleep;
The wrong shall fail, the right prevail,
With peace on earth, good will to men."

"**D**e profundis clamavi ad te, Domine," Latin for "Out of the depths I have cried to You, O Lord." So wrote the psalmist three millennia ago. Many years later, and with that same sentiment, wrote the poet as he penned the words to what would become this Christmas carol.

It had not been an easy two years for the poet. He wrote while consumed with grief over the loss of his beloved wife of 18 years, a victim of flames from an accidental household fire claiming her life while in his arms—he was unable to save her. This tragedy was followed by the serious civil war injury that nearly took his oldest son's life a year later. Finally, the poet wrote while his nation was being torn asunder by said war, tearing it apart with death, violence, and suffering like any civil war will do— quite an oxymoron "civil war" is.

But at least he was writing again after a dark depression had silenced this once prolific poet. He was now writing on Christmas morning just as the world was plunging into its darkest time of the year. Exactly one year earlier the poet wrote in his journal on Christmas morning, "'A Merry Christmas' say the children, but that is no more for me." But he was wrong, because he was writing again, and this time finding hope in his, and our, darkness.

Again, similar to the psalmist three millennia ago who said, "I wait for the Lord, my soul waits, And in His word I do hope," our poet wrote, "God is not dead; nor does he sleep! The Wrong shall fail, the Right prevail!" To wait for the Lord is to wait for His perfect will to unfold and complete itself in all its glory according to His word. The path involves a dark winter's night and the birth of a child, a lonely cross where the Child dies alone for the sins of the world, and to a victorious resurrected king returning to set up His eternal Kingdom of Righteousness.

These are words of hope for a future where Right prevails—A bright reality drowning out the darkness. These are words of peace and goodwill toward us—God's specific delight in all of us combined. These are words demonstrated by action—God so loved the world that He gave His only Son. These are words of incomparable love— The Son of God who loved us and gave Himself for us. May we delight in such words!

Grace to you and peace from God the Father and our Lord Jesus Christ,

who gave Himself for our sins, that He might deliver us from this present evil age, according to the will of our God and Father...

And may we comprehend those bells of hope this Christmas season!

Psalm 130:5

I wait for the LORD, my soul does wait,

And in His word do I hope.

DECEMBER 17

Come Thou Long Expected Jesus

By Wesley J. Livingston

Come Thou Long Expected Jesus

Come, Thou long expected Jesus
Born to set Thy people free;
From our fears and sins release us,
Let us find our rest in Thee.

Israel's strength and consolation,
Hope of all the earth Thou art;
Dear desire of every nation,
Joy of every longing heart.

Born Thy people to deliver,
Born a child and yet a King,
Born to reign in us forever,
Now Thy gracious kingdom bring.

By Thine own eternal Spirit
Rule in all our hearts alone;
By Thine all sufficient merit,
Raise us to Thy glorious throne.

By Thine all sufficient merit,
Raise us to Thy glorious throne.

Come Thou Long Expected Jesus

As I consider these timely lyrics of Charles Wesley's hymn, *Come Thou Long Expected Jesus*, I find myself overwhelmed with great joy as the Christmas season quickly draws near, but most importantly, in awe of the theological weightiness and hope in such a short song.

The anticipation of the Christmas season brings much joy to many during such a festive holiday. From fellowship to singing in the cold and wintry nights, the joy of Christmas is a memory stone that is etched into the hearts of men, women, and children alike. However, for others, this season can be a bit daunting and quite lonely as many suffer the grave emptiness of lost loved ones who have passed. For these individuals, the reality of not seeing their loved ones makes this holiday seem emotionally taxing. Loneliness, sadness, isolation, and the like are but a few descriptors of their anticipation of what's to come. But despite the present difficulty, there is greater hope of things to come.

The reality is, many people long to experience the joys of the Christmas season, not because of the gifts that are offered under a tree or singing Christmas carols from door to door, but because so many desire to be drawn into deep connection and love. This longing expectation of relationship and comfort cannot be provided or sustained by temporal means but is found in someone who is eternal in being. This longing to be loved and rescued from the present distress of this life is a common desire that all of humanity shares but rather than seeking the One who has made these provisions possible, they seek their own path and resolve.

We must come to realize that our hopes, dreams, and lives, in general, are but passing vapors —here today gone tomorrow. The only thing that truly lasts is knowing Christ and Him crucified. What great joy there is in knowing what His life, having been wrapped in flesh, means for those who are far from Him. To know that God, the Second member of the Trinity, put on flesh to draw near to the brokenhearted goes beyond what words could express. That type of love was willing to be marred so that we might be made whole. Christ's first advent made way for all in enmity with God to be made right before God (Eph. 2:1–3). This is the great joy that all who are in Christ have and remains the good news for all who are far from Him. Additionally, this good news doesn't stop here—it gets better! Not only has Christ's death made the way for us to be made right with God, but His resurrection guarantees that this life is not the end but simply the beginning.

Christ promised His bride that He would come back for her. The fact that we have a Living Hope means that there is good news, even beyond the grave. That although we may see devastation in this life and calamity in every corner of the earth—this too shall pass. For the saints in Christ, we hold onto this great anticipation of meeting our Lord Jesus in the clouds, where we will receive our resurrected bodies. This glorious outcome is only a result of a great and glorious God. This joy is found complete in Christ and not in any works that we could attempt to accomplish or attain in this life. A question to consider is, how can one's life be instantaneously turned from tragedy to triumph, from devastation to delight, from hopelessness to hopefulness? Friends, that answer is found only in the free gift of salvation offered in Christ alone. He alone can save. He alone can deliver, and He alone can give the dead life!

As you reflect upon the lyrics of this hymn this holiday season, I pray that it draws you into great gratitude for the glorious salvation we have received in Christ, and may it fill you with awesome anticipation of His glorious return when we will be with Him.

Oh, that we may grow to know Him more!

1 Peter 1:8–9

And though you have not seen Him, you love Him, and though you do not see Him now, but believe in Him, you greatly rejoice with joy inexpressible and full of glory, obtaining as the outcome of your faith the salvation of your souls.

DECEMBER 18

As With Gladness Men of Old

By Mark Nyreen

As With Gladness Men of Old

As with gladness men of old
did the guiding star behold;
as with joy they hailed its light,
leading onward, beaming bright;
so, most gracious God, may we
evermore be led to Thee.

As with joyful steps they sped
to that lowly cradle-bed,
there to bend the knee before
Him whom heav'n and earth adore;
so may we with willing feet
ever seek Thy mercy-seat.

As they offered gifts most rare
at that cradle rude and bare;
so may we with holy joy,
pure, and free from sin's alloy,
all our costliest treasures bring,
Christ, to Thee, our heav'nly King.

The Babylonians, having the Scriptures from the time of Israel's captivity, noticed the unusual star in the west which would mark the rise of the divine king foretold by God. "I see him, but not now; I behold him, but not near; a star shall come forth from Jacob, a scepter shall rise from Israel" (Num. 24:17a).

As our carol says, "with joyful steps they sped" being led surely to the one to be king of the nations. What they found was a baby! This may not have been what they anticipated, but they were ready. They had brought gifts fit for a king, and perhaps, unbeknownst to them, a Savior.

The Lord Jesus would have to grow into His kingship. As He did, and presented Himself to His nation as their king, it became clear that He had something else to do prior to taking the throne. He rejected the corrupt teaching of the Pharisees which they had used to taint the divine Mosaic law to trigger the scorn of the religious leaders of Israel. This fulfilled the Scriptures not only of a ruling and reigning righteous Messiah, but also for a suffering Savior.

The Savior grants, to all who believe in Him, deliverance from sin's penalty in hell. He has paid the price for the salvation for the whole world so that anyone who believes will receive eternal life.

In light of this, what gifts can we bring to our soon-coming king? Can we pay Him back? Never!

The price is far too high. Not only this, but payback for a gift is an insult. Our gift to Him is our worship, our fellowship, and our trust. Our gift is our will and our future returned to His loving and capable hands as we follow His guidance through our lives.

Hebrews 4:1–2, 9–11

Therefore, let us fear if, while a promise remains of entering His rest, any one of you may seem to have come short of it. For indeed we have had good news preached to us, just as they also; but the word they heard did not profit them, because it was not united by faith in those who heard.

So there remains a Sabbath rest for the people of God. For the one who has entered His rest has himself also rested from his works, as God did from His. Therefore let us be diligent to enter that rest, so that no one will fall, through following the same example of disobedience.

DECEMBER 19

O Little Town of Bethlehem

By Tom Stegall

O Little Town of Bethlehem

O little town of Bethlehem,
How still we see thee lie!
Above thy deep and dreamless sleep
The silent stars go by.
Yet in thy dark streets shineth
The everlasting Light;
The hopes and fears of all the years
Are met in thee tonight.

For Christ is born of Mary;
And, gathered all above,
While mortals sleep, the angels keep
Their watch of wond'ring love.
O morning stars, together
Proclaim the holy birth;
And praises sing to God, the King,
And peace to men on earth.

How silently, how silently
The wondrous Gift is giv'n!
So God imparts to human hearts
The blessings of His heav'n.
No ear may hear His coming;
But in this world of sin,
Where meek souls will receive Him still,
The dear Christ enters in.

O Little Town of Bethlehem

The world's most famous cities are known by their unique features and characteristics. Paris, the city of romance, is under the shadow of its iconic Eiffel Tower. Rome, the eternal city, is famous for its ancient history, Colosseum, and the Vatican. Dubai is marked by rapidly multiplying spires of glass and steel arising out of the lifeless, scorching desert sands. Rio de Janeiro sits in a basin by the ocean, rimmed by lush green hills, overseen by a towering statue of Jesus.

Bethlehem is another city known for Jesus— the real Jesus. And unlike these other world-famous cities, the little town of Bethlehem has no sizeable population or remarkable landmarks or topography. It would remain largely unknown to the world except that it was the birthplace of Israel's King David and later of Israel's ultimate King, Jesus Christ, the Savior of mankind.

In the mid-1800s, a pastor from Philadelphia named Phillips Brooks visited Israel and spent a quiet and peaceful Christmas Eve in the little town of Bethlehem. He was so moved by the experience that three years later, back in Philadelphia, he wrote a new Christmas carol about it for his church's upcoming Christmas program. Brooks gave the lyrics to his Sunday School Superintendent and organist, Lewis Redner, who composed a simple melody for the children. The result was this simple and beautiful Christmas classic about the Savior's birth.

But why sing about an obscure little town in Judah, one of thousands of otherwise ordinary dots on a map? The fulfillment of Bible prophecy is a reason to sing! The promise of Messiah's birth in little Bethlehem (Mic. 5:2) had waited over seven centuries until that fateful night when the silence of the heavenly host was broken. Not since the dawn of creation had "the morning stars" (Job 38:7) made such a glorious proclamation as our Creator, Jesus Christ, joined Himself to His creation to be our Savior. What a moment when Bethlehem, amid its "deep and dreamless sleep," became the entry point for the Light of the world (John 1:9)!

Bethlehem means "house of bread" in Hebrew, and that night the little town became host to the Bread of life Himself. This matches the third verse of the song, which says, "The wondrous Gift is giv'n! So God imparts to human hearts the blessings of His heav'n." These grace blessings, including eternal life, are guaranteed to all "meek souls" who "will receive Him" simply by faith (Hab. 2:4; John 1:12). What a generous, gracious Giver we may thank and worship this Christmas season!

John 6:51

"I am the living bread that came down out of heaven; if anyone eats of this bread, he will live forever; and the bread also which I will give for the life of the world is My flesh."

DECEMBER 20

While Shepherds Watched Their Flocks

By Dr. Arnold G. Fruchtenbaum

While Shepherds Watched Their Flocks

While shepherds watched their flocks by
night,
all seated on the ground,
an angel of the Lord came down,
and glory shone around.

"Fear not," said he for mighty dread
had seized their troubled mind
"glad tidings of great joy I bring
to you and all mankind.

"To you, in David's town, this day
is born of David's line
a Savior, who is Christ the Lord;
and this shall be the sign:

"The heavenly babe you there shall find
to human view displayed,
all simply wrapped in swaddling clothes
and in a manger laid."

Thus spoke the angel. Suddenly
appeared a shining throng
of angels praising God, who thus
addressed their joyful song:

"All glory be to God on high,
and to the earth be peace;
to those on whom his favor rests
goodwill shall never cease."

R abbinic sources make it clear that in the culture of Yeshua's day, shepherds were often held in contempt. Their work rendered them unclean and excluded them from mainstream society. While nowadays a certain romanticism is attributed to their profession, first-century Jews would have considered them highly unlikely candidates for the high honor that they were granted by the appearance of the Shechinah glory.

Those readers of Luke's Gospel who are aware of the negative rabbinic view of the shepherds might regard them as a symbol for sinners. Those who are unaware of the first-century Jewish perspective might look upon them as a symbol for the common man.

The flocks tended by the shepherds in Luke's account may have been the sheep of *Migdal Eder*. In the Jewish mindset, it was a settled conviction that the Messiah would be born in Bethlehem and the people were equally convinced that "he was to be revealed from *Migdal Eder*, "the tower of the flock." This tower was located close to the road to Jerusalem, and a passage in the Mishnah (Shek. 7.4) leads to the conclusion that the flocks that pastured there were destined for Temple sacrifices. If this view could be substantiated, it would indicate that these sheep were slated to be sacrificial animals. It would be of deepest significance if the shepherds who first heard of the Messiah's birth were watching sheep destined to be offered as sacrifices in the Temple.

The shepherds were instructed to go and find this child. However, there were many babies in Bethlehem, so how would they know which baby it was? The angel declared, *And this is the sign unto you* (Lk. 2:12). The term "sign" by itself does not require the miraculous, but minimally, it does require the unusual, something out of the ordinary. This sign contained two elements: first, a baby was *lying in a manger*; second, the baby was *wrapped in swaddling clothes*. The reference to the manger told these shepherds not to look in the private homes of Bethlehem but to look inside a cave that was used as a stable. Professional shepherds would know where these stable-caves were located.

Swaddling clothes could not be merely baby clothes, because that would not be a sign—it is not unusual for a baby to be wrapped in baby clothes. These strips of cloth gave the appearance of burial cloth. The symbolism should not be missed. On the very first day of His life, Yeshua was wrapped with the same type of cloth He would again be wrapped with on the last day of His life, showing the purpose of His birth. We were all born to live, but this One was born to die, as signified by His being wrapped in what appeared to be burial cloth.

John 1:29b

"Behold, the Lamb of God who takes away the sin of the world!"

DECEMBER 21

What Child Is This?

By Ben Coleman

What Child Is This?

What Child is this who, laid to rest
On Mary's lap is sleeping?
Whom Angels greet with anthems sweet,
While shepherds watch are keeping?
This, this is Christ the King,
Whom shepherds guard and Angels sing;
Haste, haste, to bring Him laud,
The Babe, the Son of Mary.

Why lies He in such mean estate,
Where ox and ass are feeding?
Good Christians, fear, for sinners here
The silent Word is pleading.
Nails, spear shall pierce Him through,
The cross be borne for me, for you.
Hail, hail the Word made flesh,
The Babe, the Son of Mary.

So bring Him incense, gold and myrrh,
Come peasant, king to own Him;
The King of kings salvation brings,
Let loving hearts enthrone Him.
Raise, raise a song on high,
The Virgin sings her lullaby.
Joy, joy for Christ is born,
The Babe, the Son of Mary.

T he opening question "What Child is This?" pleads with us to reflect on the wonder of the Christmas story. Who was *this* child that even His birth should warrant the celebration of millions? Why did the arrival of *this* baby incite a multitude of angels to praise God before the shepherds? The angelic announcement tells us, "For unto you is born this day in the city of David a Savior, who is Christ the Lord" (Luke 2:11). As the hymn's chorus majestically proclaims, "This, this is Christ, the King!" The Messiah, the one they had been waiting for, had finally come!

It's hard to imagine the significance of a vulnerable baby born in such a humble setting. After all, babies can't do much on their own. But this was no mere human. This was Immanuel, "God with us." His arrival truly was magnificent because it meant that God Himself had become one of us! And not only that, but as lines such as "the silent Word is pleading" and "the King of kings salvation brings" point out, Jesus did not come without purpose. Though an infant, He was destined to provide salvation to the world! So, as you hear this beloved hymn this season, consider how marvelous it is that God Himself came to us in human form, and that our Savior was here for you before He could even walk or talk.

Isaiah 9:6

"For unto us a Child is born, Unto us a Son is given."

DECEMBER 22

We Three Kings

By Dr. Daniel E. Woodhead

We Three Kings

We three kings of Orient are;
Bearing gifts we traverse afar,
Field and fountain, moor and
mountain,
Following yonder star.

O star of wonder, star of night,
Star with royal beauty bright,
Westward leading, still proceeding,
Guide us to thy perfect light.

Born a King on Bethlehem's plain
Gold I bring to crown Him again,
King forever, ceasing never,
Over us all to reign.

Frankincense to offer have I;
Incense owns a Deity nigh;
Prayer and praising, voices raising,
Worshiping God on high.

Myrrh is mine, its bitter perfume
Breathes a life of gathering gloom;
Sorr'wing, sighing, bleeding, dying,
Sealed in the stone cold tomb.

Glorious now behold Him arise;
King and God and sacrifice;
Alleluia, Alleluia,
Sounds through the earth and skies.

A t this time of year, we traditionally celebrate the birth of Jesus. In Matthew's Gospel we read of Herod the king of Judea receiving some people from an eastern land who were alerted that the true "King of the Jews" that had been born. As a result of their visit Herod and the general population of Jerusalem were very upset. Just who were these people and why was Herod threatened? God was bringing His long-awaited Messiah to the earth.

The vast majority of Jewish people, who should have been looking for their Messiah, were unaware of the birth of Christ, whereas these Gentiles, who were not God's people at that time, did seek to acknowledge this King. The same situation exists today as we anxiously anticipate His second arrival. Most are not aware of the promises of His Second Coming; but those of us who know Him look for Him to appear at any time.

Not only was Christ a physical earthly King by virtue of His lineage from David, but also by virtue of the fact that those in the world who were official kingmakers recognized Him as such. They were led by a special star which was the Shekinah Glory of God leading them. The Magi were from Media-Persia and were Persian kingmakers. Because of their well-known role as kingmakers, Herod was concerned that they were seeking his throne.

After the Babylonian Empire fell in 539 BC the Media-Persian Empire took control of that region of

Mesopotamia. Following that empire Alexander's armies conquered it for the Greeks in 328 BC. When Alexander died in 323 BC one of his generals, Seleucus Nicator, took control of the area and finally lost control of it to the Parthians in 139 BC.

Magi is the Old Persian word *magav*, which refers to a certain very wise hereditary priestly tribe of people who came from the Medes. This term is also translated as "megistanes" from which we get our term magistrates. The Magi were so powerful that historians (Herodotus) tell us that no Persian was ever able to become king except under two conditions: he had to master the scientific and religious discipline of the Magi, and he had to be approved of and crowned by the Magi. In effect, they controlled who could be king within the Mesopotamian region of the Orient.

Occupying a place of great prominence in the kingdoms of Babylon, Media, and Persia, they served as advisors to the rulers, and so the term became synonymous in many ways with being a wise man. This is how our English translations render the word *magav*. Now, some time after the birth of Jesus, some God-fearing Magi arrived in Jerusalem asking for the genuine King of the Jews so they could honor Him with their gifts and adoration.

God controls human history; and we are seeing God at work. Long ago He picked out a man named Daniel and put him in a place to influence some men so that they could arrive in perfect timing for the birth of Jesus to bestow their adoration for Him.

Interestingly, the people who should have known the great significance of the event missed it, and the people from way off who should have never guessed it could happen, arrived to worship the One who came to provide salvation to all who would accept His gift of eternal life. Israel was chosen to realize that Emmanuel, God with us, was coming to earth. He then reached out to include the Gentiles and grafted us in (Rom. 11:17). Therefore, when the King arrived, and His own people, the Jews did not realize it was their Messiah, God made sure that there was somebody there to honor Him.

And you know in our world today, people celebrate Christmas by passing around Christmas cards and giving gifts. They look at the Wise Men, but few really understand the significance of their presence before that Child. There are some of us, however, who have followed the example of the Wise Men and bowed down to the "KING OF KINGS, AND LORD OF LORDS" (Rev. 19:16b).

Matthew 2:1

Now after Jesus was born in Bethlehem of Judea in the days of Herod the king, magi from the east arrived in Jerusalem, saying, "Where is He who has been born King of the Jews? For we saw His star in the east and have come to worship Him."

DECEMBER 23

I Wonder as I Wander

By Dr. Bradley W. Maston

I Wonder as I Wander

I wonder as I wander out under the sky,
How Jesus, the Saviour, did come for to die.
For poor, ornery people like you and like I
I wonder as I wander
Out under the sky.

When Mary birthed Jesus, 'twas in a cows' stall,
With wise men and farmers and shepherds and all.
But high from God's heaven a star's light did fall,
And the promise of ages
It did then recall.

If Jesus had wanted for any wee thing:
A star in the sky, or a bird on the wing;
Or all of God's angels in heaven to sing,
He surely could have had it,
'Cause He was the King!

I wonder as I wander out under the sky,
How Jesus, the Saviour, did come for to die.
For poor, ornery people like you and like I
I wonder as I wander
Out under the sky.

I Wonder as I Wander

In all the hustle and bustle of the Christmas season it is easy to get caught feeling quiet, humbled, and even sad. This can be a wonderful thing if used to contemplate the wonderful love of our Savior. This song is certainly one of the lesser known, more melancholy Christmas tunes that has been handed down through history, and it holds a special place in my heart.

I always sing this hymn quietly to myself on a cold December evening. Bundled up in my winter gear when I can walk through the silent Colorado snowfall. Snow has an amazing effect at night. I can hear the crisp steps of my feet, but the tumbling flakes seem to mute all the other sounds. As I wander through the snowy streets of my neighborhood, I wonder along with the songwriter.

The humble circumstances in which the Lord Jesus Christ came to earth are amazing. It is too small an entrance—too inexplicably secret. Yet, these are the circumstances that He chose. As I look up at the great vaulted ceilings of the night sky and marvel at the beauty of all that God has done, the comparison becomes so amazing. I am reminded again, God doesn't do things our way, nor the way we would expect. His way, however, is always the best way. In the quietness of this winter walk I marvel and remember all the difficult and confusing situations of my life and wonder what the Lord will do to bring Himself glory even through this humble life of mine.

Hebrews 12:3

"For consider Him who endured such hostility from sinners against Himself, lest you become weary and discouraged in your souls."

DECEMBER 24

Silent Night

By Bill Harger

Silent Night

Silent night! Holy night!
All is calm, all is bright
'round yon virgin mother and child!
Holy infant, so tender and mild,
sleep in heavenly peace,
sleep in heavenly peace.

Silent night! Holy night!
Shepherds quake at the sight.
Glories stream from heaven afar,
heav'nly hosts sing, "Alleluia!
Christ the Savior is born!
Christ the Savior is born!"

Silent night! Holy night!
Son of God, love's pure light
radiant beams from Thy holy face
with the dawn of redeeming grace,
Jesus, Lord, at Thy birth!
Jesus, Lord, at Thy birth!

Silent night! Holy night!
Wondrous star, lend thy light;
with the angels let us sing
"Alleluia" to our King:
"Christ the Savior is born!
Christ the Savior is born."

S*ilent Night* is a very appropriate carol for Christmas Eve, for several reasons. It lovingly describes the wonderous occasion of the night of our Lord's birth when he was laid in a manger. How fitting that this hymn was first sung one Christmas Eve over 100 years ago.

It was composed as a poem by a young Austrian priest named Joseph Mohr in 1816 but was not immediately set to music. On Christmas Eve 1818, Father Mohr wanted it sung in service. He took it to Franz Gruber, a church musician, and asked if he could put it to music in time for the evening Mass. The church organ was broken, so Gruber composed the melody on a guitar in a few hours, and it was sung by the choir for the first time that Christmas Eve. Even today, it is said to be a tradition in Austria that the song is not sung until Christmas Eve!

While the setting of the carol evokes a beautiful pastoral scene—one that we have all come to love—the title may be inaccurate. Joseph and Mary were in Bethlehem to pay their taxes to the Roman authority ruling over Israel, and it was so crowded that we are told there was "no room at the inn." It is likely that there was a lot of noise in the hustle and bustle of Bethlehem. Mary and Joseph had no choice but to stay in a stable with farm animals, which is an unlikely place for the birth of the Eternal King who created the universe.

While it may not have been a silent night, it certainly was a holy night. If all was calm, still nothing could be brighter than the hope God gave each of us with the birth of His Son, the Lord and Savior Jesus Christ, Savior of the world.

But perhaps we ought to look more closely at these lyrics. "Round yon Virgin, Mother and Child. Holy infant, so tender and mild." A virgin mother giving birth to a holy infant? How was this possible? This seemingly odd lyric celebrates the most profound truth in God's creation. That truth is the *reason for the season* and the reason mankind has the opportunity to spend eternity with God.

Matthew 1:18 records, "Now the birth of Jesus Christ was as follows: when His mother Mary had been betrothed to Joseph, before they came together she was found to be with child by the Holy Spirit". The angel Gabriel had told Mary that it would happen this way: "The Holy Spirit will come upon you, and the power of the Most High will overshadow you; and for that reason the holy Child shall be called the Son of God" (Luke 1:35). This fulfilled precisely a prophecy given to Isaiah 700 years earlier (Isa. 7:14).

Theologians have debated these passages for two thousand years. Yet, the simple truth is that this child was conceived of a virgin by the Holy Spirit. This is the clear teaching of Scripture, so we can trust that it is true, though the mechanics of it may remain, for now, shrouded in mystery. The child was fully man and fully God. This divine conception was necessary because God needed a perfect, sinless sacrifice for the sins of the world. "Christ the Savior is born!"

It is little wonder that the night this happened—Christmas Eve—"heavenly hosts" were singing "Alleluia" (*praise God*), and "glories" were "streaming from heaven afar," causing shepherds to "quake at the sight." This was the birth of the "Son of God, love's pure light." Though the radiant beams of his glory were veiled by his newly acquired flesh, indeed he was still the light of the world and his glory would one day be seen in all the world. Indeed, this was the "dawn of redeeming grace!" Jesus was born, and he was our "Lord at His birth."

Thank you, Father, for this perfect plan! Thank you, Holy Spirit, for the miracle of this conception with your chosen virgin! And thank you, Lord Jesus, for your sinless life and perfect sacrifice! And thank you Joseph Mohr for this beautiful carol celebrating Christmas Eve—the dawn of redeeming grace.

MERRY CHRISTMAS!

Matthew 1:18–25

Now the birth of Jesus Christ was as follows: when His mother Mary had been betrothed to Joseph, before they came together she was found to be with child by the Holy Spirit.

And Joseph her husband, being a righteous man and not wanting to disgrace her, planned to send her away secretly. But when he had considered this, behold, an angel of the Lord appeared to him in a dream, saying, "Joseph, son of David, do not be afraid to take Mary as your wife; for the Child who has been conceived in her is of the Holy Spirit. She will bear a Son; and you shall call His name Jesus, for He will save His people from their sins."

Now all this took place to fulfill what was spoken by the Lord through the prophet: "BEHOLD, THE VIRGIN SHALL BE WITH CHILD AND SHALL BEAR A SON, AND THEY SHALL CALL HIS NAME IMMANUEL," WHICH TRANSLATED MEANS, "GOD WITH US."

DECEMBER 25

Away in a Manger

By David Roseland

Away in a Manger

Away in a manger,
No crib for a bed,
The little Lord Jesus
Laid down His sweet head;
The stars in the heavens
Looked down where He lay,
The little Lord Jesus
Asleep on the hay.

The cattle are lowing,
The Baby awakes,
But little Lord Jesus,
No crying He makes.
I love Thee, Lord Jesus,
Look down from the sky
And stay by my side
Until morning is nigh.

Away In a Manger

T his little Christmas Carol transports us as little children to a faraway scene 2,000 years ago, where God the Son rested in a cattle feeder beside His mother Mary.

The simple words of the "cradle song" cultivate this scene just enough to make the most important devotional point imaginable. We want, more than anything, a vibrant, personal relationship with the One born among men for the salvation of the world. We want Him near us. We want to be with Him now and forever. We love Jesus, "Who loved me and gave Himself for me," (Gal 2:20).

When you boil down the great biblical doctrines of Christian sanctification, soteriology, and even the hypostatic union for a young child to understand, the presentations must be simple and concrete yet accurate. The information we give to children has to be broad but honest, so that as they mature, the details will fill in for them on the outline they received with their ABCs. *Away in a Manger* provides such an outline in its simple verses and through its gentle lullaby tune.

The little one sings "no crib for a bed" long before thinking, "Why not?" We will grow into the answer—because there was no welcome place for the Son of God in this broken and sinful world. He was rejected in His ministry and ultimately through His death for the sins of those who rejected Him. His was a life of rejection by men but approval by the Father, and we who follow Him will know the same rejection and approval, as the New Testament repeatedly maintains (John 15:19, 17:14). It was nothing personal, perhaps, that there was "no room in the inn," but our Lord's birth circumstances fit this pattern of rejection by mankind. People are just too busy; today there's "no room in my *life*." If only they knew who Mary's baby was and what His delivery meant! Children know that the baby Jesus had to sleep "on the hay," and they will grow up learning why and what exactly it means that God's Son was born to peasant descendants of King David. He was lowly at birth but glorious for eternity according to the Father's magnificent design.

The word picture, "the little Lord Jesus lay down His sweet head," places our Lord and Savior at eye-level to a toddler. Afterall, He once was down there where a three-year-old could reach over and kiss his forehead. That's what little children do when they meet the new baby, right? This carol is for children who are a little bit older than the newborn baby Jesus. They were once there too, crying—or not—and needing a diaper change and to nurse. God the Son was born a helpless baby like all of us, and that is a big part of the wonder and mystery of Christmas.

Our cradle song switches contexts rapidly, almost like a child's attention. We move from the stable with the cattle lowing to the Lord Jesus looking down from the sky. That is so perfect! Jesus was a baby back then, historically in real time and space, and now He is at the Right Hand of the Father in glory. The childlike heart, full of the manger scene, moves to devotion toward the present reality of the exalted Christ with words he must grow into: "I love Thee, Lord Jesus." What more important devotional idea should a little Christian child learn than his appropriate response to Jesus' great love for us?

While an exhaustive grasp of God's imminence and transcendence may be beyond the reach of mature believers, a little child can think of Jesus being "up there" "looking down from the sky" and still "staying by my cradle till morning is nigh." Jesus promised to be with us always "until the end of the age" in Matthew 28:20. The sooner we start thinking of Him that way, the better.

We conclude the devotional prayer with intercession for "all the dear children" and the desire to be made "fit for heaven." What can this mean but Christian spiritual growth and sanctification? This reminds young and old that this life has a purpose and destiny in the New Heavens and New Earth. The little one who sings "Away in a Manger" is learning to pray in accordance with God's revealed will, "singing and making melody in his heart to the Lord."

Our Lord's entrance into human history is certainly the occasion for greatest rejoicing and celebration. What better way to celebrate than to reflect on our relationship with the One who came to die that we may live!

John 1:10-13

"He was in the world, and the world was made through Him, and the world did not know Him. He came to His own, and His own did not receive Him. But as many as received Him, to them He gave the right to become children of God, to those who believe in His name: who were born, not of blood, nor of the will of the flesh, nor of the will of man, but of God."

About the Authors

Bradley W. Maston

Brad and his family have served the Lord in many different capacities. He has worked teaching the Bible in South Korea, served outreach missions with at-risk youth, and has been a youth pastor to two Korean congregations. He received an MA in Biblical Theology at Channel Islands Bible College and Seminary and was mentored and built up at Holly Hills Bible Church. He completed his PhD in Jewish Studies at Scofield Bible Institute with a focus on Jewish Intertestamental Literature.

Brad is passionate about the clear teaching of God's word and building up Christian leaders. He is a board member and adjunct professor at Chafer Theological Seminary. He is also an adjunct professor at Scofield Bible Institute. For nearly a decade, Brad has been involved in Camp Arete which has a mission of teaching and encouraging young believers in middle school and high school.

Pastor Brad's messages can be heard daily on Grace Global Radio. He also heads Fort Collins Bible Church Biblical Training Program which makes seminary-level education available to anyone accepted into the program entirely free of charge. Brad is also the founding President of the Fort Collins Bible College (fcbiblecollege.com) and professor of Bible Study Methods and Church History at that institution and a founding owner of True Grace Books.

E Dane Rogers

Dane is a founding owner of True Grace Books, the pastor of Tacoma Grace Bible Church and a professor of theology at Fort Collins Bible College. After graduating from the University of Victoria, British Columbia, with a B.A. in Hispanic and Italian Studies, Dane moved to South Korea where he taught elementary and middle school English at EiE, Korea University's preparatory academy. Dane holds an MBS from Chafer Theological Seminary and is now working toward his ThM. Bible study recordings and other study materials are available at edanerogers.com and tacomagracebc.org.

J. Morgan Arnold

J. Morgan Arnold (BBA, Texas A&M University) is a graduate student at Chafer Theological Seminary. He has been the co-owner of a search engine marketing firm since 2013 and has worked at several Dallas advertising agencies as a marketing specialist since 2003. From 1994–2001, he served as a Director for the Union Gospel Mission of Seattle. For the past eight years, he has served as a men's Bible teacher for Bible Study Fellowship in Denton and Decatur, TX. He and his wife, Rocki, have been married for 30 years. They boast two grown children and two lazy Labrador retrievers. Morgan is a board member of True Grace Books.

Bill Harger

Bill Harger is an attorney practicing in the Houston, Texas area. He had a career as a professional pilot before becoming an aviation attorney. He is a student at Chafer Theological Seminary, and an Elder at Sugar Land Bible Church in Sugar Land, Texas. Bill is a board member of True Grace Books.

Benjamin Coleman

After graduating from Frontier School of the Bible with a Bachelor of Arts degree in Biblical Studies, Ben moved on to obtain both a Bachelor of Science degree in Business Administration and a Master of Accountancy degree from Colorado State University. He has served in several organizations, such as the Holland Rescue Mission and Frontier School of the Bible, gaining experience in nonprofit accounting and systems. Ben and his wife Holley have a passion for using their gifts in ways that grow them and others.

Robert Dean

Robert Dean, Jr is pastor of West Houston Bible Church in Houston, Texas, and instructor of Church history for Chafer Theological Seminary. He serves on the boards of Chafer Theological Seminary and the Pre-Trib Rapture Study Group.

Dr. Dean trained for ministry at Dallas Theological Seminary where he earned a ThM in Hebrew and Old Testament Studies before returning to earn a PhD in theological studies with an emphasis in historical theology. He also earned an M.A. in Philosophy from the University of St. Thomas (1987) and a DMin from Faith Evangelical Seminary (2002). In 1988 he was recognized as an Outstanding Young Man of America, and in 1989 was listed in the Who's Who in American Christian Leadership.

Dr. Dean is a much sought after Bible teacher both in the United States and overseas where he has ministered in Africa and Eastern Europe for more than thirty years.

Dr. Dean is the co-author of *What the Bible Teaches About Spiritual Warfare*, with Dr. Tommy Ice and *God's Powerful Promises* (both available from Dean Bible Ministries, deanbibleministries.org). He has also authored numerous theological articles which have appeared in *Bibliotheca Sacra*, the *Chafer Theological Journal*, and the *Conservative Theological Journal*, and several Bible dictionaries and encyclopedias, as well contributed articles for Tim LaHaye's *Prophecy Study Bible* and the *Popular Handbook on the Rapture*.

Matt Fehrn

Matthew Fehrn was raised in a household that loved Jesus and studied the Bible together daily. After finishing high school he served in the US Navy. He has long been a student of the Bible and has taught and led at Fort Collins Bible Church since 2014. His life experience and disciplined training at the FCBC Biblical Training Program have yielded a wealth of knowledge in biblical theology, and he passionately pursues a clear understanding of the biblical text through original language study. Matt was recognized as an elder at Fort Collins Bible Church in January of 2021. He and his wife, Rochelle, have two daughters and an amazing family.

Arnold G. Fruchtenbaum

Dr. Arnold G. Fruchtenbaum is a Messianic Jewish believer in Yeshua. He is the Founding Director of Ariel Ministries (ariel.org) and a much-respected biblical authority in evangelical and Messianic circles. Since obtaining his ThM from Dallas Theological Seminary in Hebrew and Old Testament Studies and a PhD from New York University in the late 1970s, he has taught the Scriptures globally from a Messianic Jewish perspective. His contribution to this devotional comes from his book *Yeshua* – The Life of Messiah from a Messianic Jewish Perspective.

Jacob P. Heaton

Jacob P. Heaton and his wife, Amanda, and their four children live in Thornton, Colorado. Jacob is the pastor of Fellowship Bible Church (fbcedgewater.org) which serves the Denver metro area and is on staff at Fort Collins Bible College. Jacob received his B.A. at Frontier School of the Bible in LaGrange, WY, and is currently pursuing a ThM at Chafer Theological Seminary and a M. Div. at Colorado Biblical University.

Wesley Livingston

Wesley J. Livingston is a dedicated Bible teacher at Verse By Verse Ministry International (vbvmi.org). With a deep-rooted faith nurtured in Houston, Texas, Wesley preached his first sermon at 18. Wesley earned a bachelor's and a master's degree in architecture from Prairie View A&M University and taught high school architecture.

In his quest for an expository Bible-teaching church, he discovered Verse By Verse Fellowship, where Pastor Stephen Armstrong ignited his passion for in-depth, verse by verse teaching.

In 2020, Pastor Armstrong invited Wesley to join Verse By Verse Fellowship full-time as Youth Pastor, where he received invaluable discipleship and training in expositional preaching. Pastor Wesley resides in San Antonio, Texas, with his wife and two children, faithfully sharing the gospel of Jesus Christ.

Paul Miles

Paul Miles serves as the executive director of Grace Abroad Ministries. He lives in Kyiv, Ukraine with his wife and son. They are currently displaced to America due to Russia's genocide of the Ukrainian people. Paul has a B.A. in Russian, an M.A. in Theological Studies, a DMin in Bible and Theology and is working on a PhD in Applied Apologetics. He is formulating his dissertation as a biblical and apologetic refutation of the political worldview of Russia's struggle against the West. Paul likes coffee and hates the metric system.

Mark Mills

Dr. Mark Mills earned a B.A. in Mathematics from Cedarville College, a M.A. in New Testament from Calvary Theological Seminary, and a PhD in New Testament from Baptist Bible Seminary. He is currently serving as an adjunct professor of intermediate and advanced Greek at Chafer Theological Seminary, a group leader of men at the G3 Expository Workshops, and an elder and teacher at First Baptist Church of Lindale, Texas.

Mark Nyreen

Mark Nyreen is a teaching elder at Tacoma Grace Bible Church in Tacoma, WA. He is passionate about teaching the word of God and sharing the the grace of God and eternal life in Jesus. Mark's Sunday school class recordings can be found at tacomagracebc.org.

Eric Plemel

Eric loves the Word of God and enjoys sharing it with others. Having been saved as a child, and having grown to value walking in the light of God's word, he now seeks to help others see the simplicity of knowing the Lord. He lives near Minneapolis, MN with his wife Erin and their three children. As a member of the Grace Gospel Bible Church, he serves as an elder and teaches the Scriptures. (gracegospelbiblechurch.org)

David Roseland

Before coming to Preston City Bible Church (www.prestoncitybible.org), David Roseland grew up in East Texas, a life-long student of categorical, exegetical Bible teaching. He graduated from the U.S. Military Academy at West Point in 1999 with a B.S. in electrical engineering and was commissioned as an Armor Officer.

He served for five years in the Army's 4th Infantry Division, enjoying an unusually long tenure as a platoon leader, first with tanks and then an Infantry Mortar platoon. David taught the Warhorse Bible Study in Ba'Qubah, Iraq.

Upon returning to the U.S. in April 2004, David began to transition to civilian life as a seminary student. He graduated from Dallas Theological Seminary in May 2007 with a Master of Theology in Bible Exposition.

David and his wife Krista were married at West Point, NY in 2001 and now live in Eastern Connecticut.

Luther Smith

Luther Smith (MRS, MACP, PsyD) is the Lead Counselor and owner of N(y)oo Mind Biblical Counseling, LLC & the Department Chair of Biblical Counseling at Calvary University in Kansas City, MO. He is the author of several books, including The Big Six, The Majesty In The Menial: The Doctrine of Good Works, Foundations of Counseling Biblically, Philosophical Foundations of Counseling Biblically, and The Divine Nine.

Tom Stegall

Tom Stegall currently serves as Senior Pastor at Duluth Bible Church in Duluth, Minnesota. He has authored several books and articles. He is also the director of Grace Institute of Biblical Studies and Grace Gospel Press. His radio programs Truth for Today and A Closer Look can be heard weekly on Grace Global Radio. Tom is a graduate of the University of Minnesota Duluth, Grace Institute of Biblical Studies, Moody Bible Institute, and Grace Biblical Seminary (ThM, ThD).

Jeremy Thomas

Jeremy graduated from Texas Tech University with a B.S. in Biology. Following undergraduate studies, he worked in plant physiology for five years. During this time, he attended Tyndale Theological Seminary.

Jeremy is currently pastor-teacher of Spokane Bible Church, and adjunct faculty at Chafer Theological Seminary. He is author of two books, Basics of the Faith and Galatians: Gospel of Freedom. He has also published articles in theological journals in both the US and the UK. His teaching can be found on Grace Global Radio and Beyond the Walls Ministry. He and his wife, Robin, have five children and reside in Spokane, WA.

Clay Ward

Robert Clayton Ward, M.Div., D.Min. has pastored Tullahoma Bible Church in Tullahoma, Tennessee since

July 2002. In addition to pastoring, Clay trains pastors in Sierra Leone through the ministry of Disciple Makers Multiplied, serves on the board of Chafer Theological Seminary, and teaches Biblical Exposition as an adjunct professor for Chafer Theological Seminary. Clay and his wife Amy live in Tullahoma, TN and stay busy homeschooling their six children. You can access the Bible teaching and resources of Tullahoma Bible Church at www.tullahomabiblechurch.org

Kurt Witzig

Kurt is an Associate Pastor of Duluth Bible Church in Duluth, Minnesota. His many years of ministry have focused on youth, college, pastoral, and international ministry (mostly in Africa). He is married with three sons and three grandchildren.

Dr. Daniel Woodhead

Dr. Daniel E. Woodhead is a pastor of a Pentwater Bible Church and President of Theology in Perspective. He is also the president of Scofield Biblical Institute and Theological Seminary. He has been a Bible teacher for more than twenty-five years. He earned his Ph.D. from Scofield seminary under Dr. Mal Couch and holds an MBA from the University of Detroit. He attended Hebrew University in Jerusalem and Hebrew College in Massachusetts. He has been a successful entrepreneur in the energy industry and is married with three children and two grandchildren.

Made in the USA
Middletown, DE
09 November 2023